The Roman Survey of Britain

Michael J. Ferrar and Alan Richardson

BAR British Series 359
2003

Published in 2019 by
BAR Publishing, Oxford

BAR British Series 359

The Roman Survey of Britain

ISBN 9781841713489 paperback
ISBN 9781407320007 e-book

DOI https://doi.org/10.30861/9781841713489

A catalogue record for this book is available from the British Library

This book is available at www.barpublishing.com

BAR Publishing is the trading name of British Archaeological Reports (Oxford)
Ltd. British Archaeological Reports was first incorporated in 1974 to publish
the BAR Series, International and British. In 1992 Hadrian Books Ltd became
part of the BAR group. This volume was originally published by John and
Erica Hedges in conjunction with British Archaeological Reports (Oxford) Ltd /
Hadrian Books Ltd, the Series principal publisher, in 2003. This present volume
is published by BAR Publishing, 2019.

BAR
PUBLISHING

BAR titles are available from:

BAR Publishing
122 Banbury Rd, Oxford, OX2 7BP, UK
EMAIL   info@barpublishing.com
PHONE   +44 (0)1865 310431
FAX   +44 (0)1865 316916
www.barpublishing.com

To

Professor Oswald Dilke, scholar and gentleman

CONTENTS

PREFACE

The title of this work makes a bold claim; that the Romans surveyed Britain and, by implication, probably most of their empire. We set out the evidence in the following pages.

The effort put into this study has occupied us over several years and some findings have already been published. We would have preferred to have published the rest in a few succinct papers but regrettably, the British academic establishment, apart from a few exceptional individuals, has firmly closed its mind to even considering the evidence for surveys and centuriation In Britain. The reasons are not hard to find; the basic aspects of surveying require a small grasp of simple mathematics with which many archaeologists are not comfortable. This has induced several of those who serve as referees to learned journals to prevent the reporting of any unwelcome data and observations. The problem has been compounded by the fact that much of the evidence has required an intimate knowledge of the history and geography of particular areas of the country, which is tedious to those unfamiliar with the areas in question. Despite these set-backs, we have continued to collect the evidence and now have such a body of data, together with a plausible theoretical outline of the structure of the Roman survey, that it must be put before a wider audience.

It is instructive to consider how each of us, though first working separately, came independently to the same conclusion. MJF is an architect with an interest in metrology and experience of surveying. He realised intuitively that the geometric patterns that could be detected in the modern map of Roman Britain, could not be explained other than by the Romans having surveyed the island. He recognised the major grid lines and grasped the mathematical consequences of the way they were used. AR has a science background (veterinary medicine) and research experience. He developed an interest in Roman roads and centuriation, particularly in Cumberland and the Manchester area and from a study of putative Roman survey lines in the north of England, reached the quite unexpected but unavoidable conclusion that the road alignments in Cumberland could only be explained on the basis of a very accurate survey. He identified grid and survey lines that neatly fitted with MJF's outline scheme for southern England. We "met", as it were, at Chester. We now present a synthesis of our separate studies; the text is by AR and the Figures by MJF.

It is a pleasure to acknowledge the help of those who have provided us with criticism and encouragement during this study. The late Professor Dilke was always a source of advice and encouragement and his meticulous scholarship was ever at our disposal. His wife, Margaret, has continued her interest in our work. Other friends, most notably Mr Richard Bellhouse, Dr Grace Simpson and the late Mr Tom Witherby, helped in other ways.

Michael J Ferrar, The White House Cottage, 284, Upper Eastern Green Lane, Coventry CV5 7PX.

Alan Richardson, 16, Thorpe Field, Sockbridge, Penrith, Cumbria, CA10 2JN.

October 2003

PART ONE

INTRODUCTION

In ancient times conquered peoples often had to endure the humiliation of a survey imposed by the occupying power. This could involve actually measuring the land. "I will give you Tegea…," the Delphic oracle told the Lacedaemonians, "….and her fair plain to measure out with the line." (De Selincourt 1972, 66). After the Ionian revolt the Persians re-surveyed the Greek lands in *parasangs,* the Persian measure, to emphasise the Greek servitude (De Selincourt 1972, 402) and it is well documented that the Romans surveyed conquered territory.

In this report we set out a body of evidence that forced us to conclude that the Romans did in fact survey Britain, and make an accurate map furnished with a grid very similar to that of the modern Ordnance Survey. The reasons for believing this must have happened were given by Davies (1998) who concluded, "...Roman road designers would have used dead reckoning, both to provide the required bearing and information about the….landscape…this information would have been used to provide *maps, of true scale* (our italics) from which road alignments would have been designed."

Our evidence has come mainly from the disposition of Roman road alignments and centurial *limites* and from the relative geometric positions of forts and towns. The study has required a great many observations and involved scale drawing, trigonometry and some simple statistics. But this rather scientific approach was made without forgetting the historical context of the Roman invasion and settlement, or the writings of earlier Greek geographers such as Eratosthenes and Diodorus Siculus, or later ones like Marinus of Tyre and Claudius Ptolemy. With such a mixture of cartography, history and mathematics, it has required an effort to avoid a circular argument.

Our methods have centred on scale drawing; MJF being a professional in that discipline, and the computer spreadsheet. To avoid cluttering the thesis, we have not attempted to summarise completely the literature on ancient map-making nor to speculate more widely than our conclusions will strictly allow. We have rather constructed a sequence of argument that shows why the angles that certain roads make to the cardinal points of the compass indicate the existence of a Roman map with a grid. We have then suggested how the survey was probably carried out and the map used to plan the province. We stress the religious dimension for the simple reason it forced itself upon us. The later sections report further findings on centuriation in Britain and suggest that the survey extended to the Scottish Lowlands and was used in the planning of both the Hadrianic and Antonine frontiers. Finally, we shall discuss our findings and make suggestions for further research.

We have tried to make the text readable by separating much of the raw data and its mathematical treatment to the appendices. This will enable our results to be checked by those who wish to examine the data for themselves. Throughout the text, wherever we have referred to feet and miles, the Roman dimension is intended, the Roman foot, the *pes monetalis* of 11.65 inches and the mile of 5,000 Roman feet. The *actus* was 120 Roman feet and typically a *centuria* was an area 20 *actus* square. We shall, however, also use the term *centuria* to mean a linear measure of 20 *actus*. This is not ideal, but the frequency with this dimension occurs in the landscape is such that if the term *centuriae* is not used with the qualification here stated, a new one must be invented.

***

PART TWO

ALIGNMENT ANGLES OF CERTAIN ROMAN ROADS AND CENTURIAL *LIMITES*

The significance of certain angles

The major clues pointing to a Roman survey of Britain can be found in the angles that many Roman road alignments make to the cardinal points of the compass. They have certain characteristics that require a little initial explanation.

Whereas we are familiar with measuring angles in degrees, 360° to a circle and 90° to a quarter circle (right-angle), the ancients expressed the same idea with reference to a right-angled triangle, with the angle expressed in terms of the proportion of the length opposite the angle to that along the side. Thus, the angle made by the diagonal of a square to one side was 1/1. The most familiar right-angled triangle has sides in the proportion 3:4:5. The long side (5) facing the right-angle is the *hypotenuse*. The two other angles may be expressed in terms of the ratio of the sides of the triangle. This is basic trigonometry. In Figure 2.1 which shows a 3:4:5 ratio sided triangle, the *Tangent* of angle *b* is the opposite over the adjacent, 3/4; the *Sine* is the opposite over the hypotenuse, 3/5 and the *Cosine* is the adjacent over the hypotenuse, 4/5. When a capital "A" is placed before the term, it expresses the value of an angle whose ratio is known, thus, *Atan, Asin, Acos*. For example *Atan* 1/1 is 45° and is found in the triangle that makes half a square. We shall speak of the *Atan* frequently in this work.

This system had certain very practical advantages because setting out angled lines over long distances is notoriously prone to error and working in degrees, as done today, requires very accurate modern instruments. With the basic equipment available in the field to the Romans, namely measuring roads and the cross staff, or *groma*, the best way was to make right-angled triangles with sides in simple whole number proportions. This reduced the number of angles that could be conveniently used but it did ensure reliability and simplicity for partly trained assistants.

These right-angled triangles with sides in *whole number* ratios thus have angles with *Tangents, Sines* and *Cosines* that are fractions with whole numbers above and below the line, like 2/3 or 3/8. Such fractions are called *rational fractions*. The ancient Greeks determined all this and the Romans were quite familiar with it (Heath 1921). So, wherever in the landscape we find man-made features, like roads, that relate to each other or to the cardinal points of the compass by angles with *Tangents, Sines* and *Cosines* that are rational fractions, we may suspect that they result from some somebody working with right-angled triangles whose sides are in whole number ratios.

Foss Way

The most striking Roman road in southern Britain is the Foss Way. Previous researchers have shown it to be clearly laid out on a straight line between Ilchester and Lincoln, but close examination of the map reveals that it comprises several small sub-alignments that connect at *alignment nodes*. The inclination of its mean line to the cardinal points of the compass is about 30 degrees E of OS grid N, but the angle cannot be determined with complete accuracy by ruler and protractor because we do not know for certain where the mean line's precise course is. This is an important consideration because the angle was chosen for good reason, but, unless measured very accurately, we cannot draw any firm conclusions about it. To define the line trigonometrically from its end points presupposes that we know exactly where the surveyors' end points actually were; but we do not. We have, however, the alignment nodes and these allow the angle to be defined by the mathematical method known as *linear regression*, whose basis is explained briefly at the end of this section.

From the OS 1:25.000 maps, 37 alignment nodes on the Foss Way were identified, together with two ends chosen at Lincoln cathedral and Axminster. Straight road sections meeting by curves were projected on the map and their intersection taken as the alignment node. These are listed in Appendix 1. The data were entered onto a computer spreadsheet and the correlation coefficient found to be 1.0 and the *slope* to be 0.6. This means that the points are actually on, or evenly scattered about, a straight line inclined E of OS grid N by an angle whose *tangent* is 0.6, or 3/5. In degrees, the angle is 30.96°. This figure is without any obvious significance, whereas the *Tangent* is eloquent of the line's geometry. The Foss Way's mean line is the hypotenuse of a right-angled triangle whose other sides are in the ratio 3:5. See Figure 2.2. This is virtually the same angle as that seen at Florence between the neighbouring centuriation and the *kardo maximus* of the city, as observed by Hardie (1965) (J. Peterson personal. communication.). The coincidence is significant.

In setting out the Foss Way line, Roman engineers appear to have made a triangle whose other sides (in the proportion 3:5) were aligned *along* the cardinal points of the modern OS grid. They could define NS and EW lines by reference to the sun's path across the sky, but to use the precise angle *Atan* 3/5 to connect two distant points, they must have known *at the outset* the locations of each end of the hypotenuse. In reality, the sites were probably defined by the line and did not exist prior to the line

3

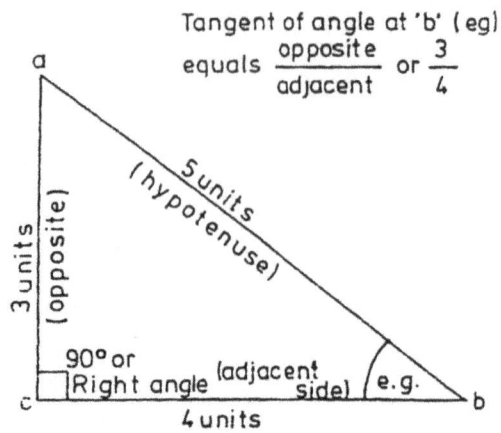

Tangent of angle at 'b' (eg)
equals $\frac{opposite}{adjacent}$ or $\frac{3}{4}$

a

3 units
(opposite)

5 units
(hypotenuse)

90° or
Right angle
c   4 units

(adjacent
side)

e.g.

b

THE 3:4:5 RATIO SIDED TRIANGLE

Fig 2.1 (left): Basic trigonometry

Fig.2.2 (below): The mean line of the Foss Way forming the hypotenuse of a 3:5 right angled triangle

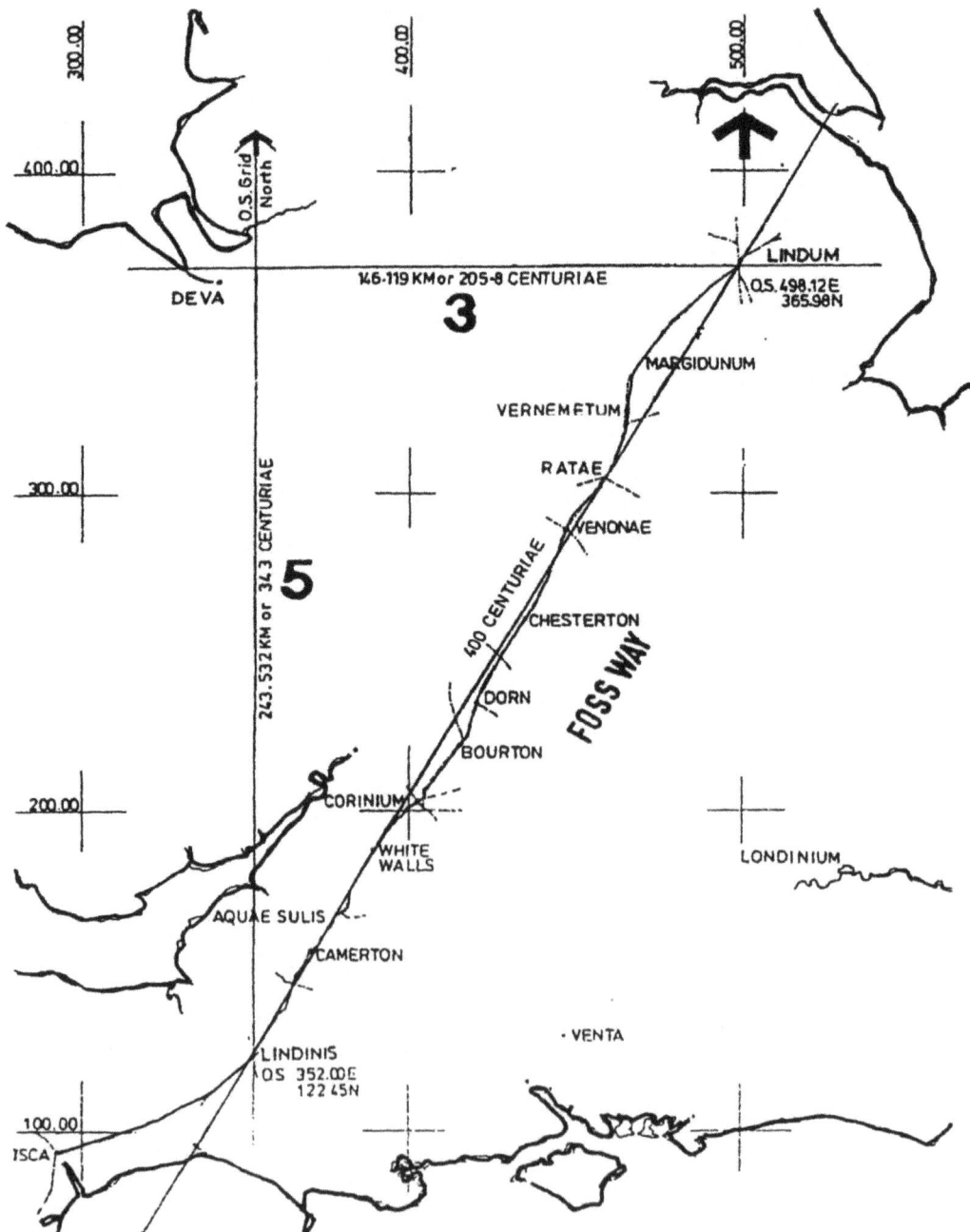

300.00

400.00

500.00

400.00

O.S.Grid North

DEVA

146.119 KM or 205·8 CENTURIAE

3

LINDUM
O.S. 498.12 E
365.98N

MARGIDUNUM

VERNEMETUM

RATAE

300.00

243.532 KM or 343 CENTURIAE

VENONAE

5

400 CENTURIAE

CHESTERTON

FOSS WAY

DORN

BOURTON

200.00

CORINIUM

WHITE WALLS

LONDINIUM

AQUAE SULIS

CAMERTON

· VENTA

LINDINIS
OS 352.00E
122 45N

100.00

ISCA

4

being set out. But the intervening country must have been surveyed and the resulting plan must have enabled the road planners to mark upon it a line that was the hypotenuse of a right-angled triangle. It is easiest to imagine this as a line running across a grid of squares and cutting through every third and fifth intersection. See Figure 2.3. The important point is that the angle is related to OS grid N, a modern cartographer's contrivance, probably because in Gloucestershire and Wiltshire true N, determined by the methods of the *agrimensores*, solar or stellar observation, is virtually the same as OS grid N. This is a crucially important matter to which we shall return.

Stane Street

This road has been much studied because its first alignment from London Bridge to Ewell in Surrey is accurately aligned on Chichester, which it eventually reaches after several deviations. The Roman bridge over the Thames lay just east of the present structure at about OS 532.85E 180.30N, while the road alignment node just east of Chichester's east gate is at OS 486.45E 104.78N. These grid references were entered onto a computer spreadsheet and the differences in eastings (*e*) and northings (*n*) between each end found by subtraction. Since the alignment was the hypotenuse of a right-angled triangle, where *e* and *n* were the other sides, *Atan e/n* gave its angle to OS grid N and the Pythagorean theorem gave the length. The intervening distances are therefore 46.40 km. EW and 75.52 km NS, giving an alignment *Tan* 46.40 / 75.52 = 0.614, virtually 0.6. This is the same angle as the Foss Way's, but W of S as opposed to E of N. The hypotenuse (road alignment) is 88.6 km. See Figure 2.4.

Certain roads in NW England

Four roads in NW England, detailed in Table 2.1, further illustrate the point; King Street, Cheshire, is aligned *Atan* 3/5 W of N; Ribchester – Slaidburn, *Atan* 3/5 E of N; Manchester – Castle Shaw, *Atan* 4/5 N of E; Middlewich – Worleston, *Atan* 2/5 W of S.

Table 2.1
Inclination to OS grid North of some Roman roads in the NW counties.

Road	Between	Tangent	
King Street, Cheshire	361.20E 386.35N – 383.20E 349.40N	0.6	3/5
Ribchester - Slaidburn	363.45E 440.10N – 371.25E 452.55N	0.6	3/5
Manchester – Castle Shaw	384.70E 397.89N – 399.85E 409.76N	0.8	4/5
Middlewich - Worleston	370.55E 366.00N – 366.60E 356.17N	0.4	2/5

Ilkley to Adel

The road from the fort at Ilkley to Adel, north of Leeds, provides another example together with evidence about the nature of the survey grid. The Ilkley fort stands south of the Wharfe at OS 411.6E 448.00N. The road leaving it for Adel may be traced south-eastwards along Cowpasture Road and then along the edge of Ilkley Moor as the *Ebor Way*, whose massive kerbs and metalling proclaim a Roman origin. The line given by Percival Ross (1918) is almost certainly not correct At Yeadon its line is marked by *Street Lane* and at *Cold Harbour* (OS 422.25E 444.55N) the line shifts clearly towards Adel. Of course one cannot be certain about the precise location of the node but using a spreadsheet to convert km. to Roman units, as shown in Appendices 2 and 3, this alignment was found to be the hypotenuse of a triangle whose other sides are coincident with the OS grid lines. Moreover, their lengths approximated closely whole numbers of standard Roman agrimensorial units, 10.4 (NS) and 15.0 (EW) *centuriae*. The alignment angle of this road section is thus *Atan* 2/3 S of W. It is very significant that the dimensions of other sides of the triangle appear to be in standard agrimensorial units for it suggests that the road was planned with a grid of such dimensions. See Figure 2.5.

Low Borrowbridge to Carlisle Roman Road

Similar features can be detected in the lay out of Roman roads that are not straight throughout their courses. This is well illustrated by the road between the fort at Low Borrowbridge, in the upper Lune valley of Westmorland, and Carlisle. This 40-mile route described Percival Ross (1920) is not straight like the Foss Way but has two main alignments, one running due

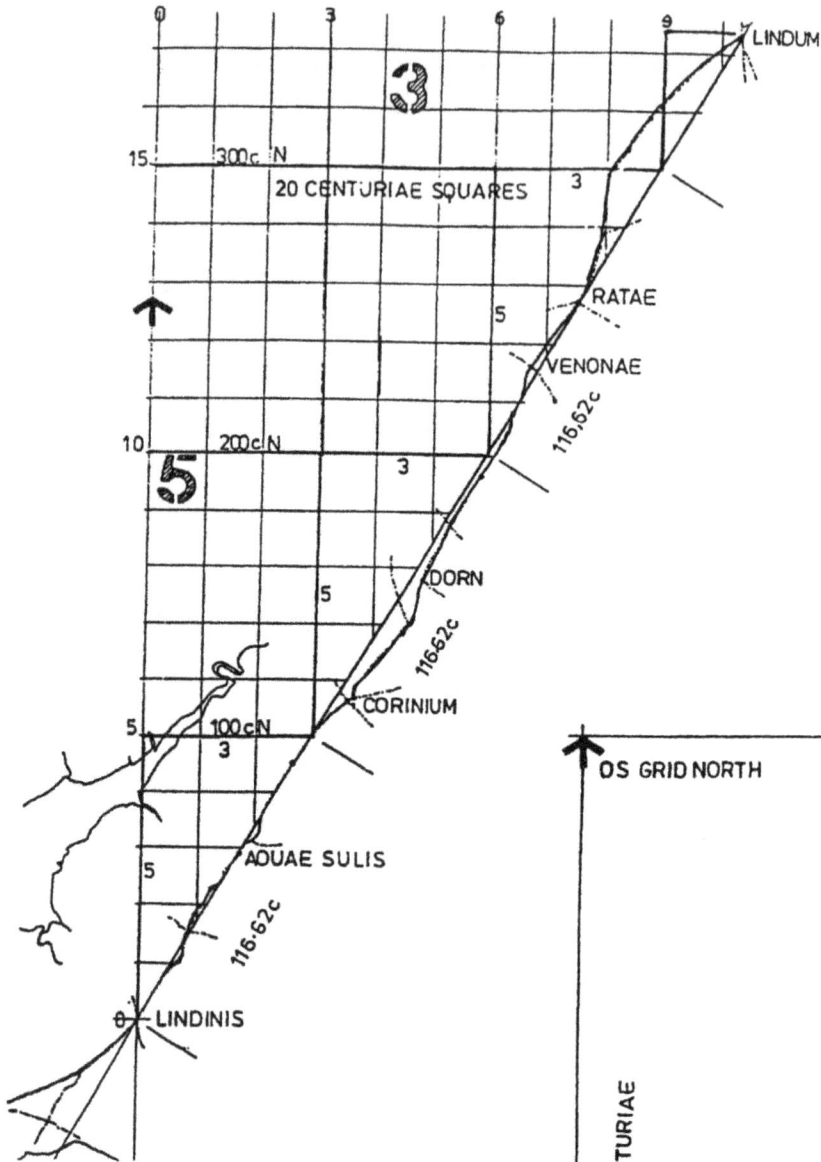

Fig 2.3 (left)
The mean line of the Foss Way
In relation to a 20 *centuriae* grid

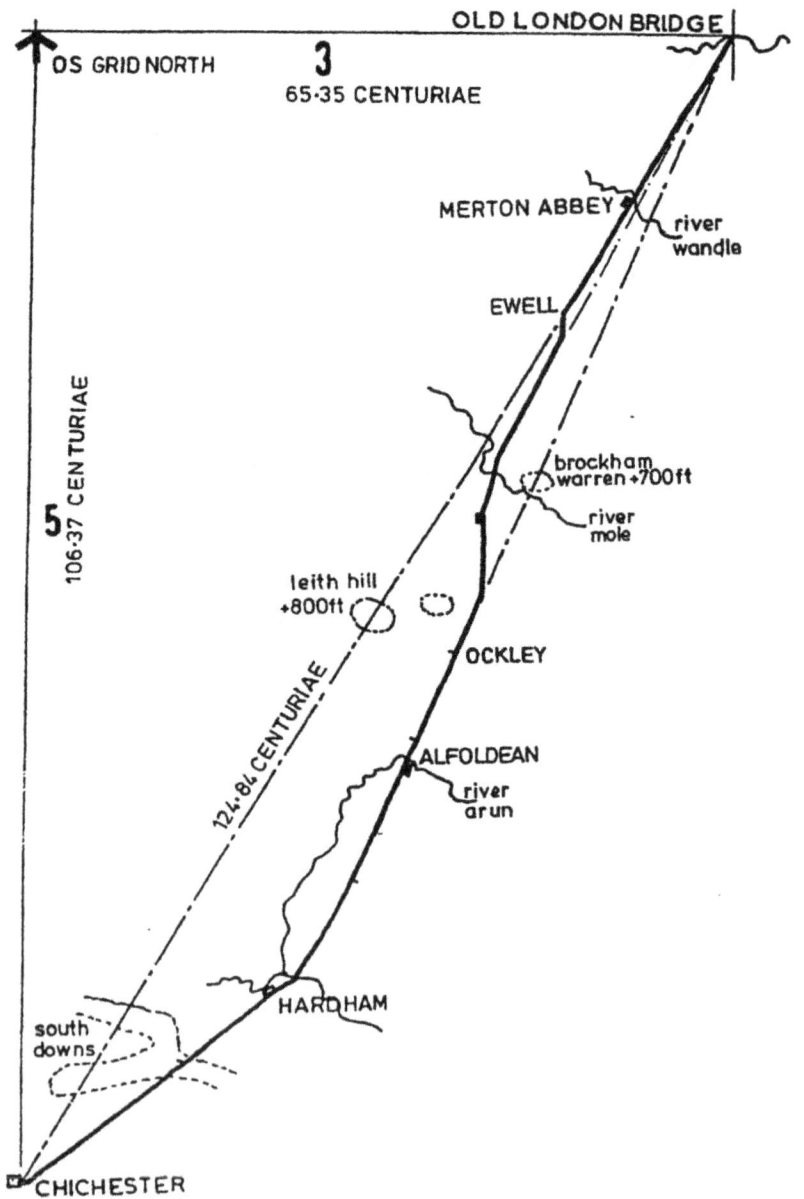

Fig 2.4 (right)
Stane Street, Sussex, mean alignment 3/5 W of S

6

north from Low Borrowbridge to Reagill and a second from thence to Carlisle. Each has sub-alignments in the middle that take the actual road course westwards before regaining the original line.

Using trigonometry and scale drawing, the *Tangent* of the angle made by each separate sub-alignment to OS grid N, and its length, were determined as stated above from the nodes identified on the OS (1:25,000) map. The main alignments are shown in Figure 2.6 and the sub-alignments listed in Table 2.2. Their OS references are given in Appendix 4.

Table 2.2
Alignment nodes between Low Borrowbridge and Carlisle

	R. miles	Tangent - fraction	
Alignment one			
L. Borrowbridge	-	-	
Roundthwaite Nth	2.0	0.02	1/50
Howenook Pike	4.0	0.19	1/5
Ewe Close	2.5	0.29	3/10
Alignment two			
Reagill	2.3	0.04	1/25
Gilshaughlin Wood	5.4	0.49	1/2
Brougham	4.0	0.71	7/10
White Ox Farm	2.7	1.05	1/1
Inglewood Cottage	7.9	0.25	1/4
High Hesket	0.8	0.47	1/2 ?
Scalesceugh	4.0	0.52	1/2 ?
Carleton	3.0	0.64	16/25
Gallows Hill	1.5	0.87	9/10
Carlisle cathedral	1.1	1.15	8/7

Alignment 1, from Low Borrowbridge fort to Reagill Grange, runs northwards along the OS grid meridian. The first section is now lost beneath the motorway but its line runs (*Atan* 1/50 E) to just north of Roundthwaite where, to avoid Orton Scar, it swings westward (*Atan* 1/5), to just west of Howeknowe Pike. It then turns to regain the meridian at Ewe Close. These two sub alignments meet at 359.90E 510.07N, though the causeways meet by a curve. From Ewe Close, the road bears *Atan* 1/25, very slightly west to Reagill where it joins the second main alignment (2). The mean value of the eastings of the points about the meridian is 360.96E.

Now the shift to alignment 2 at Reagill is not upon a hilltop or any point of vantage from which a beacon fire might be seen. On the contrary, it is in the shallow valley of the Low Wood Beck where the view to the north is blocked by rising ground. Penrith Beacon Fell, a presumed surveying point for this road, cannot be seen until one is further north. There is no obvious topographical reason why this spot was chosen for a shift of alignment. The second alignment leads off at *Atan* 1/2 W of N and runs for some five miles (*The Street*) to Gilshaughlin Wood where the road swings further west to Brougham. Thereafter, road curves west of Beacon Fell, straightens out and passing Old Penrith fort, makes for High Hesket where it falls in again with the alignment of the *Street*. From High Hesket to Carleton the road more or less holds to alignment 2 but at Gallows Hill, just south of Carlisle, it again shifts westward to the city, leaving alignment 2 to pass to the east.

Because for much of the way from Gilshaughlin Wood to High Hesket the road runs well to west of alignment 2, one cannot be quite sure whether it was intentionally related to that alignment. To resolve this we again resorted to linear regression on the alignment nodes between Reagill and Carlisle. The correlation coefficient for all the nodes proved to be 0.99, virtually a straight line and the probability tables gave a value of $p = < 0.001$, highly significant. We may safely say that throughout its length, the road was intentionally related to alignment 2. The slope was precisely *Tan* 0.5, that is 1/2, W of N. The angle in degrees is 26.56°, a value that has no significance, unlike the value of the *Tangent*, which shows that in conceptual terms at least, the line is the hypotenuse of a right-angled triangle.

Now, as in the case of the Foss Way, to connect two points by a line at an angle to the OS meridian whose *Tangent* is an exact fraction (1/2) the road planners must have known the precise two-dimensional relationship of Reagill and Carlisle *at the outset*

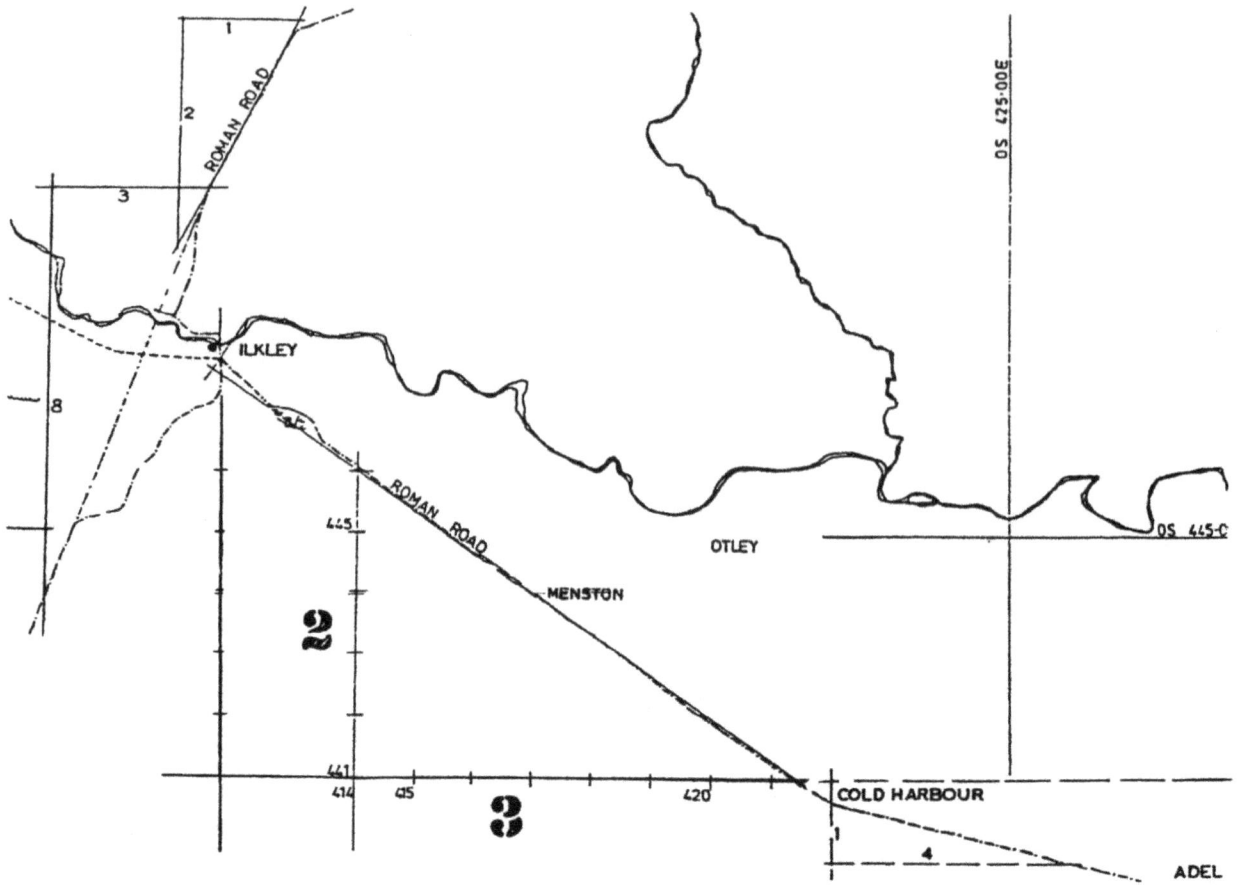

Fig 2.5 (above)
Roman road from Ikley to Adel, aligned 2/3 S of E

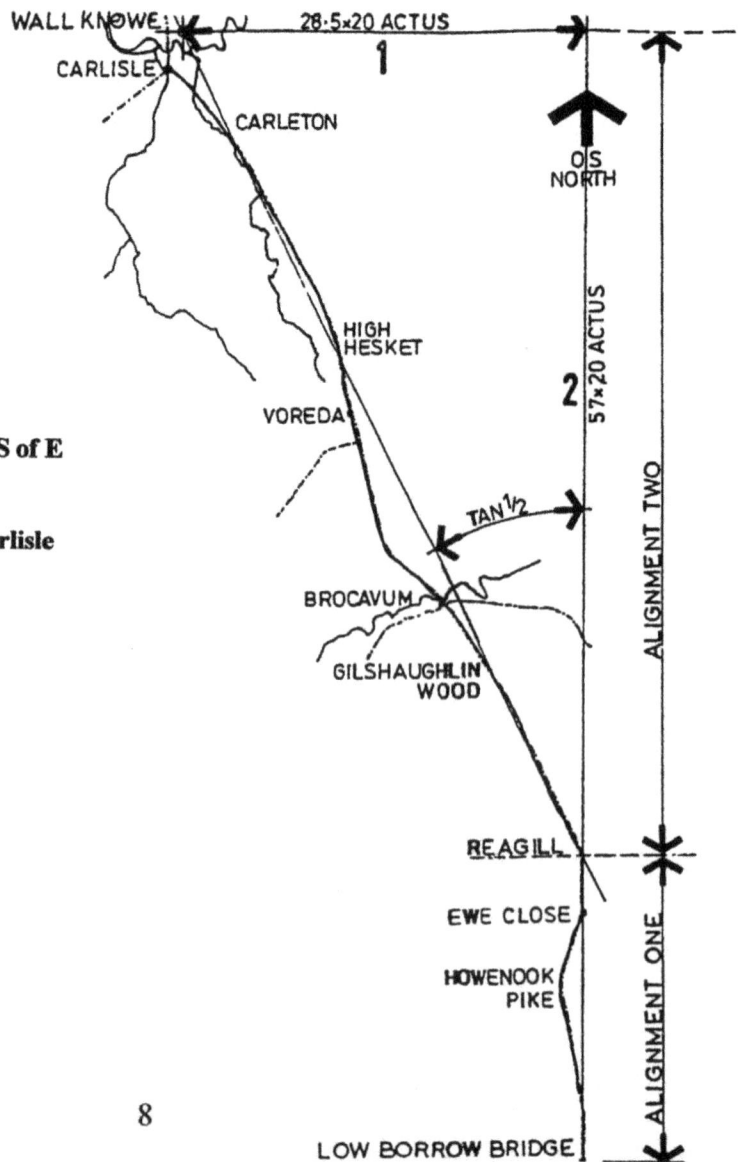

Fig 2.6 (right)
Roman road from Low Borrowbridge to Carlisle
Aligned ½ W of N

and again this could only have come from a scale plan upon which the points were spatially defined. This could only have been drawn after a survey and would explain why the shift of alignment at Reagill is south of the village on the slope down to the Low Wood Beck and out of sight of Penrith Beacon. It was made close to a grid line intersection. There never was a need for a fire beacon or similar contrivance since the proposed road course was marked on the map by joining grid-line intersections at Reagill to a point just east of Carlisle. (The reason for the point being just east of Carlisle will become clear). Everywhere on the ground, the line of the causeway could have been set out from the plan by measurement from the survey marker posts at grid line intersections. Thus we have a major Roman road of some 40 miles whose lines are based upon a geometric plan but whose actual route is modified locally to avoid difficult ground (i.e. Orton Scar) or to take in an important point (Old Penrith).

Roman roads in the southern counties

Further studies have revealed that several Roman roads in other parts of the country are also aligned to the cardinal points of the OS grid by angles with *Tangents* of rational fractions. Of course, some are small fractions, such as tenths and twenty-fifths, and it might be thought that to argue the significance of such tangents is to stretch a point too far. We shall therefore list a selection from different parts of the country with quite obvious rational fractions. The reason for choosing Devon and the eastern counties will become clear.

Eight road sections in Lincolnshire, Essex, Kent and Devon were studied. Straight sections were selected and the OS grid references of seven points along the course were subjected to linear regression. The grid references are listed in Appendix 5 and the results summarised in Table 2.3. In the case of Tillbridge Lane, Lincoln, it was quite obvious from the map that the road ran at *Atan* 1/3 N of W because it could be seen crossing the OS grid squares precisely in that way, cutting through each northing at a point three squares west of the previous one. Likewise, Wragby Road, Lincoln, could be seen leaving the city at *Atan* 4/7 N of E.

Table 2.3
Inclination of some Roman roads to OS grid North.

(c = correlation coefficient, s = slope, 1/s = reciprocal of slope)

Road	c	s	1/s	Inclination (Atan)
W. Coggeshall to Stanway, Essex	1.0	5.67	0.18	Probably 1/5 N of E
Marks Tey to N. Witham, Essex	1.0	1.09	0.92	1/1 W of S
Tillbridge Lane, Lincoln.	1.0	2.85	0.35	1/3 N of W
Wragby Rd., Lincoln.	1.0	1.74	0.57	4/7 N of E
Peddars' Way, Norfolk.	1.0	0.43	2.33	3/7 W of N
Woodensburgh to Dover, Kent	0.95	0.11	9.83	1/10 N of W
Canterbury to Dover, Kent.	0.99	0.79	1.26	4/5 W of N
Honiton towards Exeter	1.0	2.25	0.45	4/9 N of W

Further evidence of roads having been laid out on a standard agrimensorial grid comes from two roads in Sussex; London – Lewes (Margary 14) and London – Brighton (Margary 150). See Figure 2.7 Each road has two main alignments meeting at a node, and each alignment is parallel to that of its neighbour. Table 2.4 shows OS references of the nodes and the *Tangents* of angles (*Tan e/n*) that the alignments make to grid N. With very little variation, both alignments north of the nodes incline *Atan* 0.2725 W of N while those south of the nodes incline *Atan* 0.271 E of N. The mean is 0.2718, or 3/11. Direct measurement from the OS 1:50,000 map shows that the northern alignments are 10 *centuriae* apart and the southern alignments are 18 *centuriae* apart.

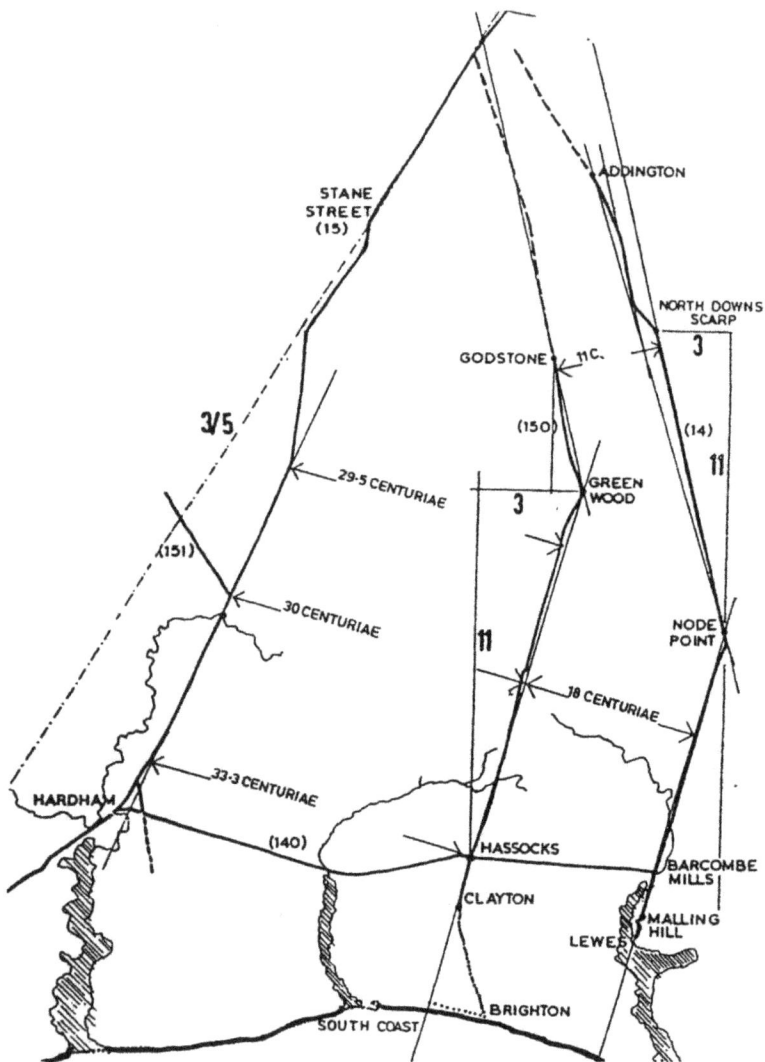

Fig 2.7 (left)
Parallel Roman roads in Sussex

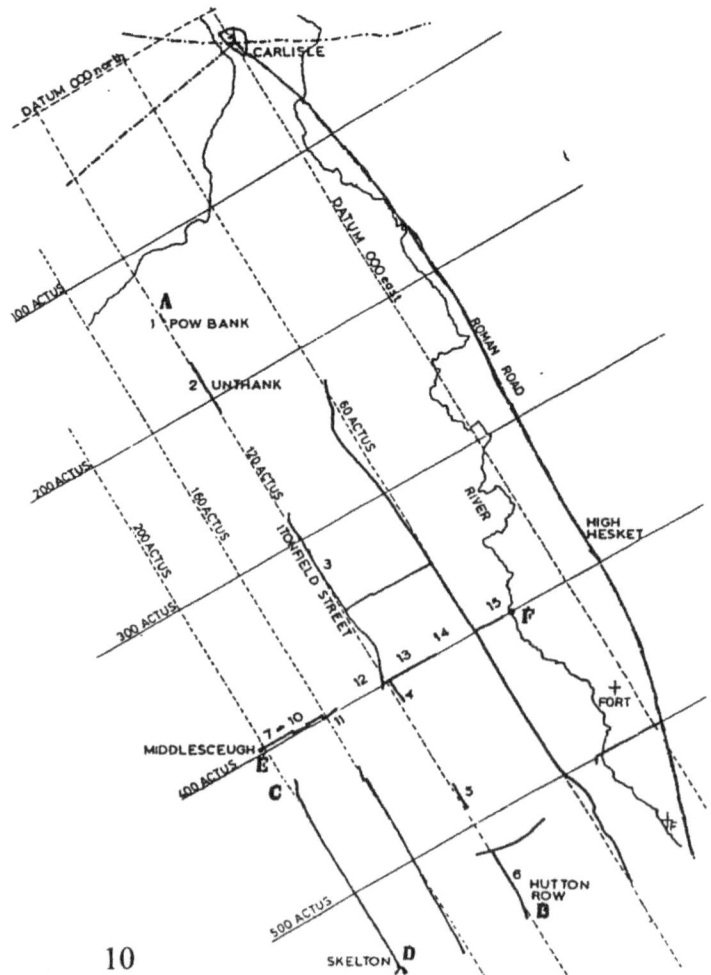

Fig 2.8 (right)
Centurial *limites* south of Carlisle

10

Table 2.4
Alignment Angles of Two Sussex roads

Road and node	OS reference	Tangent		Length in miles
Margary 150				
Godstone	534.95E 151.63N			
Green Wood	537.49E 142.28N	0.272	W of N	6.55
Clayton	529.29E 112.21N	0.273	E of N	21.0
Margary 14				
Addlington	538.61E 164.92N			
B2188 at Weald Way	547.98E 131.58N	0.280	W of N	23.4
Malling Hill	542.49E 111.61N	0.262	E of N	13.4
	Mean Tangent	0.2718		

Centuriation
Until recently evidence of centuriation in Britain has not been welcome to the academic community. Nevertheless, we shall cite evidence of four centuriation systems aligned to the OS grid by angles with *Tangents* of rational fractions.

Centuriation at Manchester
Crofton (1905) first proposed centuriation at Manchester but for many years his suggested scheme did not attract any attention. After the publication of Dilke's work on the *agrimensores* (Dilke 1971), Richardson (1983), updated Crofton's model in the light of Dilke's work and of certain new observations, particularly an intermittent series of field boundaries on a straight line that almost certainly followed a *limes*. The putative grid's alignment has now been determined from the 1848 6-inch map by reference to a hedgerow line, which formed a hypotenuse to map's edges. Thus, 597 mm of hedgerow line corresponded to 558 mm of the map's EW axis, so *Cosine* 558/597 = 0.9346, or 20.82° N of E. This is *Atan* 0.38, virtually 0.375, or 3/8. See Part 5.

Centuriation in Norfolk
Peterson (1988, 1998) has presented evidence of an extensive system of centuriation north and south of Norwich. From a statistical analysis of modern field boundaries shown on the OS map sheets he concluded that the *limites* were aligned 11.077° W of OS grid N. This angle is *Atan* 0.193, or just 0.007 less than *Atan* 0.2, or 1/5, the difference being only 0.4°. Recently, Prof. Frere has described essentially the same system but giving its EW axis a bearing of 83.5° E of *true* (not grid) N (Frere, 2000, 351). The NS axis is thus 90 – 83.5 = 6.5° W of true N. Now, at the middle of the eastern edge of OS map 144 (Norwich) true N is 2.53° W of grid N, so Frere's NS axis is inclined 6.5 + 2.53 = 9.03° W of grid N. The difference between the two estimates is 1.77°. We suggest the true angle is *Atan* 1/5, or 11.3° W of OS grid N. (See Part 5.)

Centuriation in Cumberland
Richardson (1982, 1986, 1998) has suggested centuriation in the Inglewood Forest north of Penrith and at Hayton east of Carlisle. In the Inglewood area, the clues arose from the disposition of several discontinuous sections of modern road in the parishes of Hesket and Calthwaite. They fell on three alignments, two parallel and one crossing at right angles. The parallel alignments, AB and CD, were exactly 80 *actus* apart; (i.e. four standard *centuriae*) with another road, not quite parallel, half way between. The transverse line (EF) was closely associated with nine sections of modern road forming a more-or-less through-route, with one break, from Middlesceugh to a ford on the R. Petteril. This line was 400 *actus*, that is 20 standard *centuriae*, room for exactly four *quintarii*, from a parallel line through the conjunction of Hadrian's Wall with the confluence of the rivers Eden and Caldew at Carlisle. Where lines AB and EF intersected, in Braithwaite, there were the significant place-names, *Streethead, Street Field* and *Itonfield Street*. These features are shown in Figures 2.8 and 2.9, the latter including many modern field boundaries that clearly fit the centurial grid.

Hayton (OS 350.8E 457.8N) is a village five miles east of Carlisle. It sits upon a lane running EW with another, known as *How Street*, parallel to it at 20 *actus* (one *centuria*) to the south. Both were shown on a map of 1704 before the land was enclosed.

11

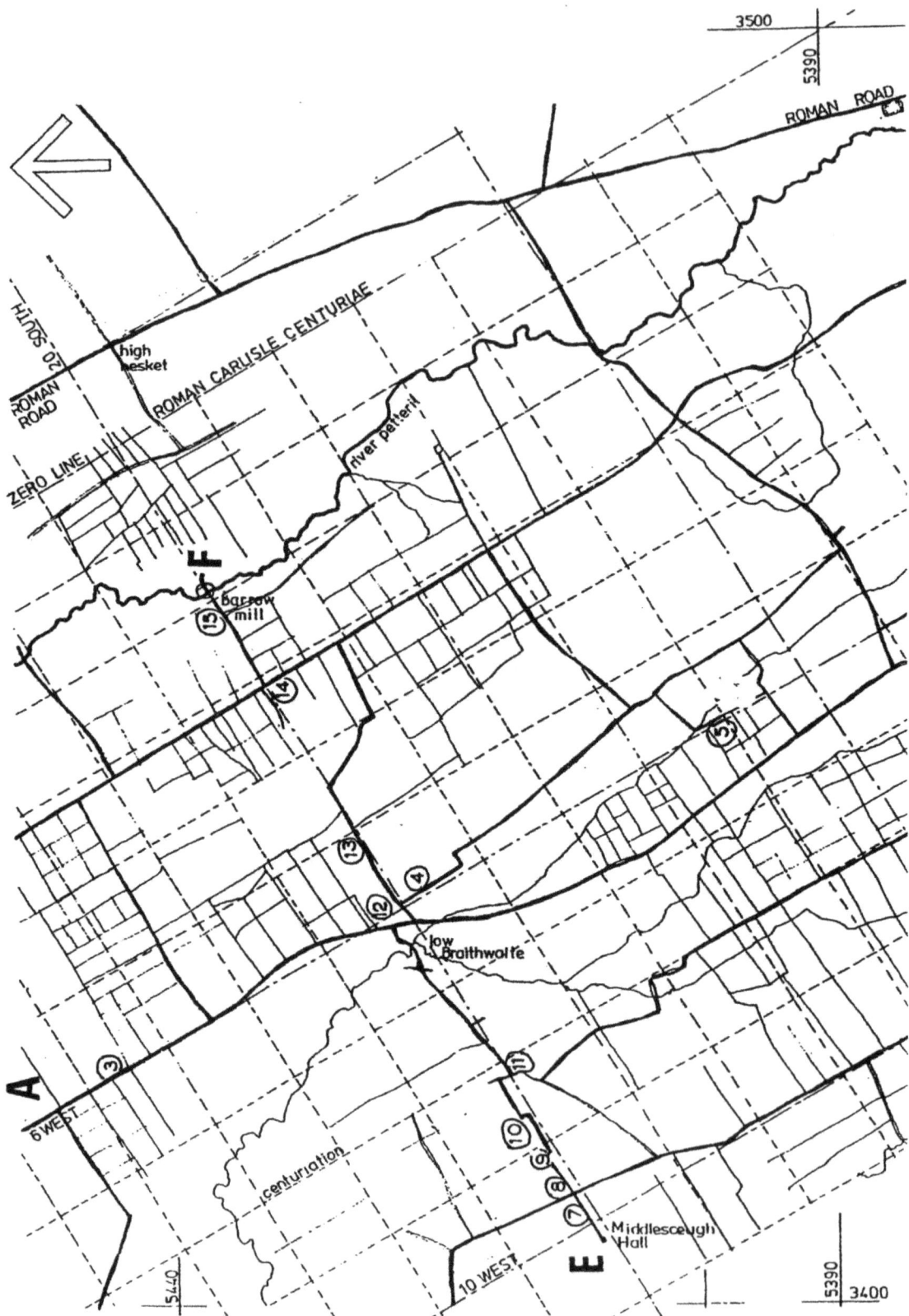

Fig 2.9: Centurial *limites* near Old Penrith, Cumberland:
limites marked by broken lines: modern lanes picked out in bold: modern field boundaries parallel
with *limites* are shown

(Graham 1907, 43). This putative Hayton centuriation is clearly aligned on the OS grid cardinal points, How Street actually lying along northing OS 577.0N. This is a typical arrangement according to the *Corpus Agrimensorum* (Dilke, 1971, 86).

On the other hand, the alignment of the Inglewood centuriation, along line AB, when measured by a protractor was about 30 degrees W of grid N. This method of measurement, however, is crude so the angle was determined by linear regression. Appendix 6 lists the OS grid references at each end of the separate lanes lying on the alignment, together with those of the series of lanes crossing at right angles (line EF). The correlation coefficient for points on AB was 1.0 and the slope 0.6, or 3/5, corresponding to an angle of 30.96° W of N, the very same angle by which the Foss Way inclines E of N and Stane Street W of S. The coefficient for line EF was 0.99 and the slope was 0.572, not 0.6, though the discrepancy is only 0.03. This reflects the wider scatter of the points along line EF.

A common datum point for the Cumberland *limites* and the Reagill – Carlisle road line

Thus we have the *limites* in the Inglewood Forest aligning *Atan* 3/5 W of N and the Reagill – Carlisle road aligning *Atan* ½ W of N. The obvious question arising was whether there was a datum point common to both lines, which would infer that the same grid used for both.

Inglewood line EF is 20 *centuriae* south of the Wall's crossing of the R. Eden, and cuts line AB at 343.10E 542.26N on *Street Field*, Braithwaite. From this intersection, scale drawing revealed there would be another intersection near the Stanwix fort. A computer spreadsheet, modified to take account of the *Atan* 3/5 angle, was used to pin-point it exactly. (See Appendix 7 for the formulae.). A point 20 *centuriae ultra* and eight *centuriae dextra* the *Street Field*, Braithwaite, intersection was found just east of Stanwix fort, on a hillock called Wall Knowe (OS 340.67E 557.35N).

Further calculations (See Appendix 8) then revealed that when the Reagill – Carlisle alignment was projected, it cut the same northing (557.35) at Wall Knowe, just 30 metres west of the Inglewood *limites* intersection at 340.64E. Thus the Inglewood *limites* and the putative road map grid lines coincided at Wall Knowe; the 30 metres discrepancy is insignificant. This point is 57 *centuriae* N and 28.5 *centuriae* W of the Reagill alignment node, which is highly significant because it demonstrates again that the common agrimensorial unit defines the *Tangent* of alignment 2, (28.5/57 = 0.5, or ½). Moreover, How Street, Hayton, running along northing 557.00, is 10 *actus*, or half a *centuria*, south of Wall Knowe and neatly fits into the putative map grid.

Most significantly, Wall Knowe is on the same easting as Chester cathedral, the site of the legionary fortress, which suggests the grid may have extended between Chester and Carlisle. This is a crucial observation to which we shall return in the next section

There can be little doubt that in Britain many Roman roads and centuriation systems are aligned to the cardinal points of the OS grid by angles with tangents of rational fractions, almost certainly as a consequence of their being planned on a grid of squares aligned in the same way as the OS grid. So far as the area south of Carlisle is concerned, the same grid appears to have been used to plan both the main road and the centuriation.

The significance of the alignment angles of roads and *limites* to OS grid N

A question of great importance, however, immediately arises from these observations; namely the distinction between OS grid N and the geographical true N, for the two are not the same. The difference is a consequence of the way maps are made and for the explanation it is necessary to say something of map projections, a subject with which Greek and Roman map-makers were quite familiar (Dilke 1985).

Map projections

Maps must be flat, but the earth is round. The Greeks knew this, though they took the earth to be a perfect sphere whereas we know it is flattened towards the poles and has some unevenness elsewhere. From the spherical model they drew a number of logical conclusions. Lines of latitude are parallel but lines of longitude converge towards the poles. Therefore a degree of latitude in terms of NS distance on the earth's surface is constant whereas the further north we go from the equator each degree longitude describes a shorter EW distance. At any point on earth's surface there is a particular ratio of distance per degree longitude to that of latitude and the ancients knew this to be the *Cosine* of the latitude: 1 (Harley and Woodward 1987, 141).

To deal with this problem in mapping large areas, Claudius Ptolemy (*c.* AD 90 - 168), in his first projection, regarded the northern hemisphere as a cone with straight, rather than curved, longitudinal lines (Dilke 1985, 78). But we must remember that he was drawing on the work of several distinguished predecessors active before the Roman conquest of Britain. This projection was reasonable for large-scale world maps but it meant that a rectangular map suffered EW distortion at its northern (top) end. On the other hand, for most practical purposes, this distortion was negligible. For mapping "prefectures and

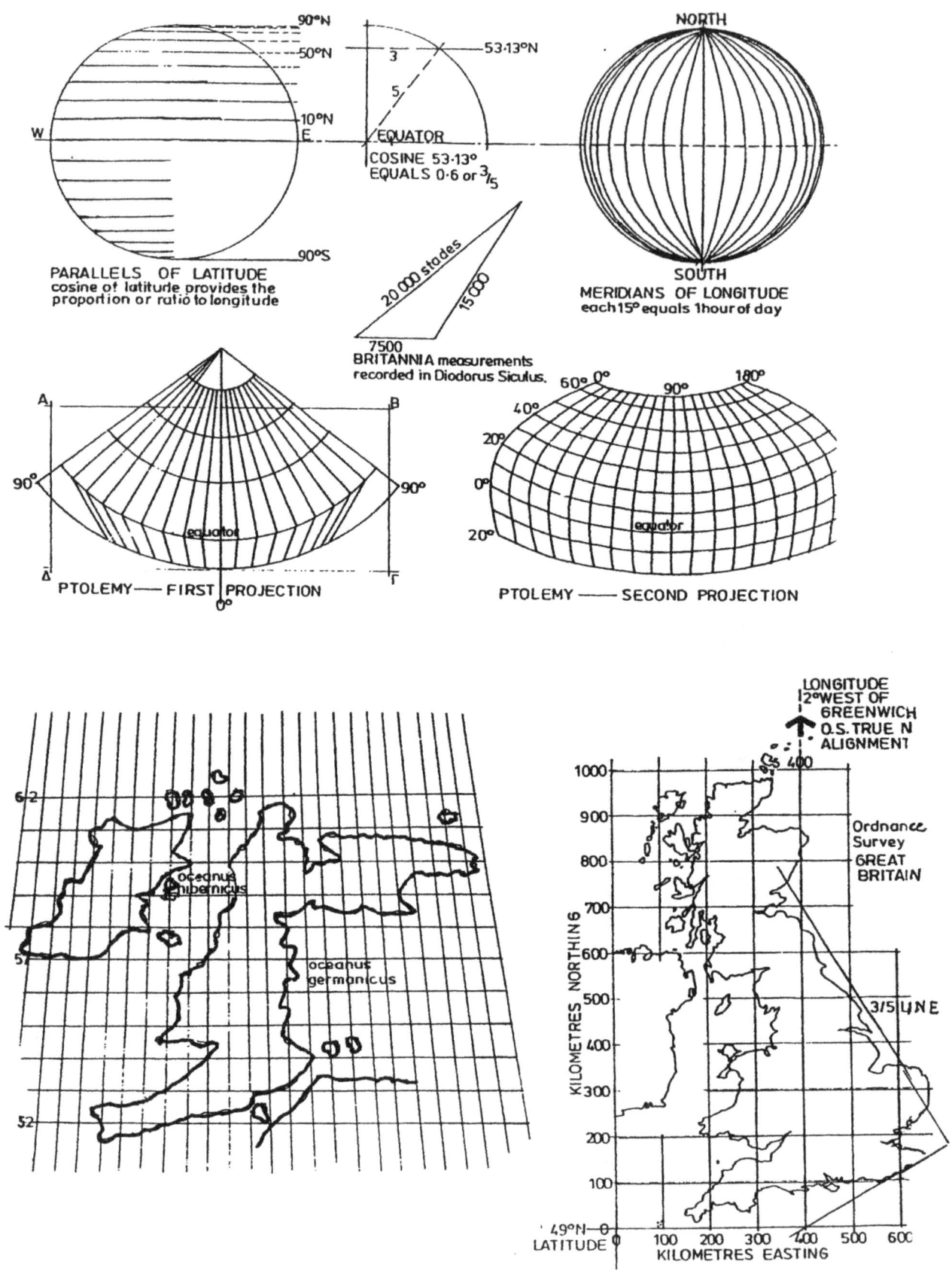

Fig 2.10: Map projections:
Top of page shows Ptolemy's projections in relation to a spherical earth, with an inset giving Britain's dimensions according to Diodorus Siculus. Below left is a map of Britain reconstructed from a certainly corrupt mediaeval document of Ptolemy's *Geographia*. Below right is the modern OS grid.

14

provinces" he wrote, "...nor will it make much difference if in these maps we use parallel meridian straight lines instead of curved lines, provided we keep the proper proportion of the meridian degrees marked on... the equator, to those in the middle of every map." (Stevenson E.L. 1932, prologue). In effect, he advised surveyors to find the province's mid latitude and mid longitude and then adjust the longitudinal (EW) distances to the mid latitude. This produced a flat map with a rectangular grid whose longitude lines were closer together than the latitudinal lines, but with the *appropriate proportion*, noted on the map. For example at 60° N the *Cosine* of the latitude is 0.5 so the lines of longitude would be spaced on the map at intervals that were half of the latitude intervals. See Figure 2.10.

The resulting map would have longitudes that were parallel but at the northern edge they would be *outside* the converging, true longitudes. For relatively small regional maps this was not, as Ptolemy wrote, a major problem. The Ordnance Survey dealt with it in essentially the same way, choosing as the mid longitude of Britain the meridian two degrees W of Greenwich (OS 400E) running north through the country from Poole Harbour to Berwick upon Tweed. This line was made N for the whole map, which was then marked with a regular orthogonal (square) grid aligned on it. West of OS 400E, true N is inclined eastwards (1.5° in West Wales) while east of it, true N it is inclined westwards (2.53°in East Norfolk). Northings, overlying latitudes, pose no problem.

Roman alignments in the east and the west of England

Table 2.3 showed that roads all over the country were aligned to OS grid N, not true N, by angles with *Tangents* of simple rational fractions. The difference between grid and true N is scarcely detectable for several miles either side of the mid easting (400.00E) but in the eastern and western districts it is greater. Therefore, comparing the rational fractions of the *Tangents* to grid N and true N, in the east and west of England should indicate the preferred meridian, because the simpler fractions should apply to the one actually used by the road engineers.

The comparison was made for alignments in Cumbria, Devon and East Anglia, using the deviation of true N from grid N as given on the OS map sheets.

1. In Norfolk, where true N is 2.53°W of OS grid N, the *limites* are aligned *Atan* 1/5 (11.3° W of grid N) and therefore at 8.77 W of true N. The *Tangent* of this angle is 0.154, or 77/500.
2. Likewise the Peddar's Way, Norfolk, is aligned *Atan* 3/7 or 23.02° W of grid N. This is 20.49° W of true N, or *Atan* 0.374, or 187/500.
3. At Carlisle true N is 1° E of OS grid N, so the Inglewood *limites* are angled 31.96° W of true N. The *Tangent* of this angle is 0.62, or 31/50, rather than 3/5.
4. Likewise, the Reagill-Carlisle road line is aligned exactly at *Atan* 1/2 W of Grid N but at *Atan* 26/50 (0.52) of W of true N.
5. In the southwest, the alignment of the road leaving Honiton for Exeter is *Atan* 2.25, or 9/4 (E of Grid N), or 66.04°. True N, here, is 1.02° E of grid N so the road inclines to true N by 65.02°, or *Atan* 2.15, which cannot be expressed as a simple fraction; the nearest value being 100/47, or 2.13.

Therefore in the NW and SE we have alignments that relate by rational *Tangents* to true and grid north as shown in Table 2.5.

Table 2.5
Tangents of alignment angles to local true N and OS Grid N

	Tangent as a rational fraction	
	True North	*OS grid North*
Norfolk *limites*	77/500	1/5
Peddar's Way	187/500	3/7
Cumberland *limites*	31/50	3/5
Reagill – Carlisle road	26/50	1/2
Honiton – Exeter road	100/47 approx	9/4

There can be no doubt that the simpler rational fractions relate to OS grid N rather than to true N. They are therefore far more plausible; indeed one might almost say that the *Tangents* relating to true N are not rational fractions at all, since they stretch the definition of that term to breaking point.

Conclusion

This state of affairs can only mean that across the whole country the Romans used the same grid, aligned as the OS grid, whose N coincided with true N at the country's mid longitude. It follows that the centre line of the Roman grid must have been about OS 400E. The facts that the Ilkley - Coldharbour, Yeadon, and the Reagill – Carlisle road alignments formed the hypotenuses of triangles, whose other sides were multiples of 20 *actus*, indicate that the grid was of 20 *actus* squares, the standard agrimensorial type. The perpendicular distances between the main alignments of the two Sussex roads, London to Brighton and London to Lewes, are consistent with this interpretation.

Note on linear regression

Linear regression is a statistical means of assessing to what extent two variables are correlated. The best example of the principle is the spring balance used to weigh vegetables. The length of the spring is directly proportional to the weight placed upon it, so plotting on a graph the spring's length against various weights gives a perfectly straight line. If, however, one were to plot the height of children against their ages, one would not get a perfect line because children vary; yet the overall statement that a child's height correlates with its age might still be true. Mathematicians have developed linear regression to deal with this problem. The details need not concern us, but the method finds the best straight line relating two data sets and tells us how close the correlation is. A *correlation coefficient* of 1.0 means the data points relate to a straight line. The nearer the coefficient is to 1.0, the better the fit. The *slope* is the angle that the line makes to the graph's axes and is expressed as the *Tangent* of the angle. Probability tables tell us to what extent the result is due to chance. It is thus an ideal method to define the angle of a set of OS grid reference points that appear to be in a straight line i.e., the alignment nodes of the Foss Way. The slope value is much more reliable because it is based on all the data points and not just the two at each end.

****

PART THREE

ANCIENT CARTOGRAPHY, ROMAN

SURVEYING AND THE ROMAN MAP OF BRITAIN

We must now consider how the Romans might have made their map, bearing in mind what we know of ancient map-making and Roman surveying methods. For a full review of ancient cartography, see Harley and Woodward (1987).

Greek maps

We have referred to the method devised in antiquity, of making a flat map of a curved surface by straightening out the lines of longitude. There is good reason to believe that this was not an innovation of Claudius Ptolemy, but rather a practice established before his time, (Harley and Woodward 1987, 130 - 148). The ancients knew this would make no practical difference to a "regional map" and their reasoning was sound so far as it went, but it created problems with the scale for maps covering large areas. The distance per degree of latitude and longitude would depend on the estimate of the earth's circumference. If, for example, the world were thought to be 360,000 miles round, each degree latitude would be equal to 1,000 miles. It is, of course, much smaller. Eratosthenes (*circa* 275-194 BC) calculated it to be 250,000 *stades,* but later changed it to 252,000 *stades* (Diller 1948, 7). Scholars are not certain which of the various *stades* he used for his calculations but since his observations were made in Egypt, he was almost certainly working in terms of the Egyptian *stade* of 157.8 metres; so in Roman measure, his circumference was 26,893 miles, or 27,000 in round figures. This gave a distance of 74.7, say, 75 miles per degree of latitude. It seems the Romans liked this; Pliny thought the dimension had divine approval (Diller 1948, 7).

Eratosthenes placed Britain between 50° N and 62° N with a latitudinal centre at 56° N (Gossellin 1883) where the lat-long ratio (*Cos* lat: 1) would be 0.56, or in fractional terms 11:20, the ratio later recommended by Ptolemy for the British map. The distance per degree longitude was thus 0.56 x 75 = 42 Roman miles. On this basis, the map of Britain would have parallel latitudes marked at 75-mile intervals and parallel lines of longitude at 42-mile intervals, but with the map marked with the correct proportion. Posidonius (*circa*. 150-135 BC) had, however, calculated the earth's circumference to be 180,000 *stades* and in the early second century AD, Marinus of Tyre and Claudius Ptolemy accepted this (Stevenson 1932). But by then, Britain was mapped and we shall suggest that the evidence points to the Roman surveyors of Britain having worked to the model of Eratosthenes. He and Posidonius were the only authorities on the matter who could have informed Roman mapmakers of AD 43.

Roman surveying

Outside the Greek tradition of academic geography and cosmology, the Romans had developed a surveying technology that owed much to Greek and Etruscan ideas but which was utterly practical in purpose. Their surveying method actually measured the land and was intrinsically associated with its exploitation and subjection to government, and their map, or *forma*, was not, like a modern map, a document merely descriptive of the land surface. The technique required a datum point of origin (*tetrans*) from which a perfectly orthogonal grid of straight lines was set out using the *groma*. A line could be set as far as the eye could see and by knocking in posts at intervals it could cross both hill and dale. By working outwards from the *tetrans* along the major lines (*kardo maximus* and *decumanus maximus*) and by careful cross sighting, a network of posts could cover the landscape in a grid pattern. Large hills or features that obscured the view could be worked round, or intermediary posts made to define the line until the correct intervals for the markers could be established. In short, the landscape had a grid imposed upon it rather as the archaeologist imposes a grid upon his excavation; the lines were defined first and then the natural features, such as rivers, or important places like towns, could be drawn in their correct positions. Rivers, for example, would be defined by the points at which they crossed *limites*, as the fragments of the Orange cadaster show (Dilke 1971, 170).

There is thus an important distinction to be drawn between the actual measuring and mapping of land, and *centuriation*, which involved setting out boundaries from a given point and dividing the land into plots, though the technique and tools were the same. Many hundreds of square miles could be surveyed, or centuriated, with considerable accuracy, as a system of at least 200 kilometres extent in North Africa demonstrates (Dilke 1987, 212) and there is no reason to doubt the Roman ability to make scale maps of such areas. Julius Caesar initiated a project to map the world that was continued by Agrippa under Augustus but never finished (Dilke 1985, 41-53) perhaps because being based on accurate measurements, the exercise proved too costly or too tedious for the harassed successors of the first emperor.

Historic background to the Roman survey of Britain

In the century before the invasion, the Romans, at both official and unofficial level, must have built up a store of information

ORIGINAL SURVEY POINTS
AND SURVEY PLANNING LINES

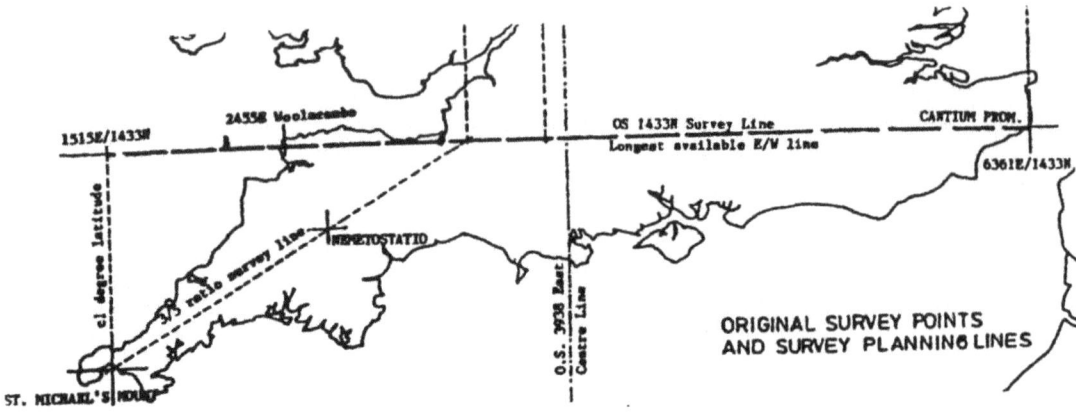

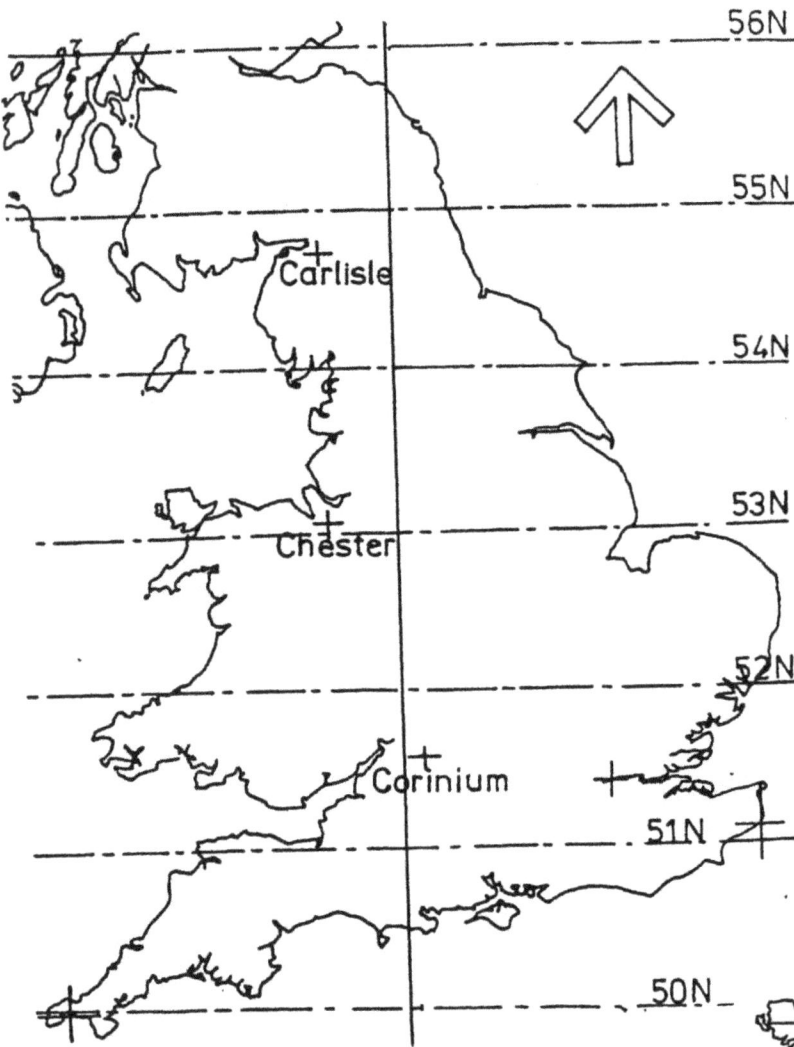

Fig 3.1 (left): Latitudes of Britain according to Eratosthenes.

Fig 3.2 (above): The suggested main lines of the Roman survey with (below right) grid lines at 20 Roman mile intervals

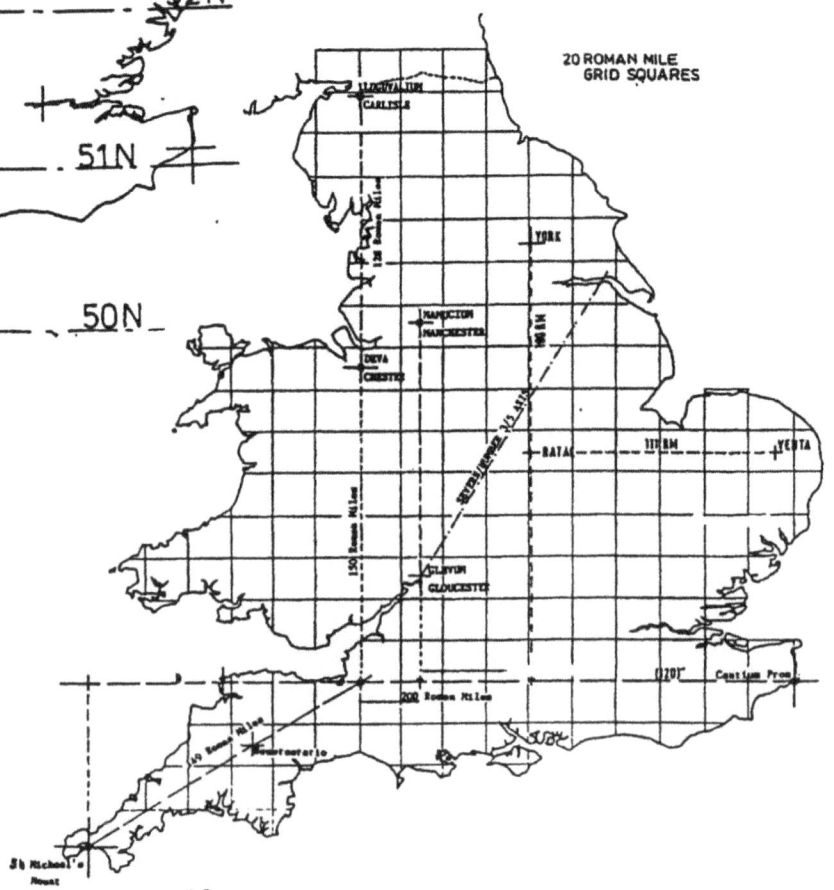

on Britain from academic texts, spies and merchants. By AD 43, they had a considerable corpus of geographical literature ranging from Eratosthenes and earlier Greek writers down to the recent work of Strabo (*circa* 63 BC –23 AD). From the latter's 17 books the military surveyors would have learned that Britain's shape was triangular with one point at the narrowest part of the Channel (Aujac 1987a, 174). The south coast in particular would have been well explored and it is quite likely that latitudes had been measured using the post method of Pytheas of Marseilles (Aujac 1987, 151); indeed, Pytheas's data may have been available, though is unlikely that prior to Agricola's expedition they were sure of anything northwards of latitude 56° N. Figure 3.1 shows the latitudes of Britain according to Eratosthenes.

Immediate post invasion survey and the establishment of the mid longitude

The invading force, then, almost certainly had a map based on Strabo, as well as some data on latitudes and longitudes. But after the landing a military surveying team would have started a new survey with the aim of establishing the mid longitude and latitude for the island, or at least that portion of it intended for the province. Without a reliable map showing important natural features and centres of population, the conquest and exploitation of the territory would have left much scope for error, misinformation and fraud. The latter was not a small matter; the younger Pliny for example, when governor of Bythinia, asked Trajan for a survey in order to keep a check on contractors (Radice 1978, 213).

Knowing from Strabo that Britain's shape was a triangle, the surveyors would have recognised the point at the narrowest part of the Channel, the South Foreland just east of Dover, which they dubbed *Cantium Prom* (OS 636.10E 143.30N). This place already had been described by Julius Caesar as the place where ships from the continent usually landed (Handford 1951, 135). It could be linked directly to Gaul and was therefore the obvious zero point for the survey. Their next step would have been to establish accurate NS and EW base lines, as required by standard agrimensorial practice. At *Cantium Prom* the direction of NS would be found by reference to the sun's path and a line at right angles to it could be made to stretch westwards.

The next task would be to place a series of posts at intervals along this line (OS143.30N), viewing across the post tops to maintain the line's direction. Progress was probably about 12 miles a day, just as in marching, so that in a little over three weeks they would have reached west coast. The line was probably measured in miles and perhaps marked off in 10 or 20-mile units. This parallel happens to be the longest EW line available across southern Britain, just skirting the north coast of Devon and finishing at Woolacombe. This circumstance may be purely fortuitous but one cannot help thinking that it may already have been known to the *agrimensores*, thanks to some previous exploration. A line a little further north would have ended at Burnham on Sea, 60 miles to the east on the Somerset coast, and a line further south would have had to start at Romney Marsh. These two lines are of similar length but the Dover parallel is much longer.

At some point along this EW base line, they would choose the location for the main NS axis and the mid longitude of the province; indeed, the two were probably the same. From that point, a network of secondary survey lines in grid pattern would be extended north and south of the EW base line. The choice of the mid longitude was not quite straightforward because the Cornish peninsula, aligning south-westwards had to be taken into account. The difficulty was probably resolved by simply extending the secondary lines, which were themselves marked at intervals, and then cross linking them to extend the grid. South and west of Salisbury plain the grid would enter Devon and Cornwall.

It is here that the grid line that we have already identified in relation to Wall Knowe, Carlisle, and Chester (OS 340.60E) assumes a new significance; it is 200 Roman miles west of *Cantium Prom*. From OS 340.60E 143.30N, the grid was extended south, probably for 75 Roman miles, one degree of latitude (Eratosthenes), to a parallel just north of St Michael's Mount (OS 029.90N).

Another line was then probably driven westwards to near the Mount itself at OS 151.50E. This extension was 127.63 miles, making the EW distance from *Cantium Prom* to St Michael's Mount 327.63 miles. The halfway point of this EW dimension may have been selected for the province's mid longitude, that is 327.63 / 2 = 163.81 miles west of *Cantium Prom*. But the most significant fact is that 160 Roman miles west of *Cantium Prom* is OS 399.51E, within half a km of the OS 400.00N, the line defining OS grid N, and this, we suggest, was chosen for the mid longitude, thus explaining why the Roman grid was aligned virtually the same as the OS grid. The whole number of Roman miles between the eastings of *Cantium Prom* and the Chester-Wall Knowe line (200) and the putative mid longitude (160) suggests the main survey lines were measured in miles. They were probably set out as shown in Figure 3.2 and their eastings and northings are given in Appendix 10. The other lines, set out parallel and at right angles at regular distances in an orthogonal grid, would thus define the spatial relationships of native towns and natural features in southern Britain and permit the drawing of an accurate and practically useful map complete with co-ordinates. The planning of roads thus became a relatively simple matter of setting design lines across the country by connecting up grid line intersections, leaving the engineers to make necessary local amendments for the actual course of the causeway.

The northward extension of the survey – the probable mid latitude

Chester cathedral (fortress site) lies at OS 366.60N, 150.8 miles north of the EW base line. This is almost 2 x 75 = 150 Roman miles, which on Eratosthenes's model would be two degrees of latitude. The true datum was almost certainly 0.8 miles south of

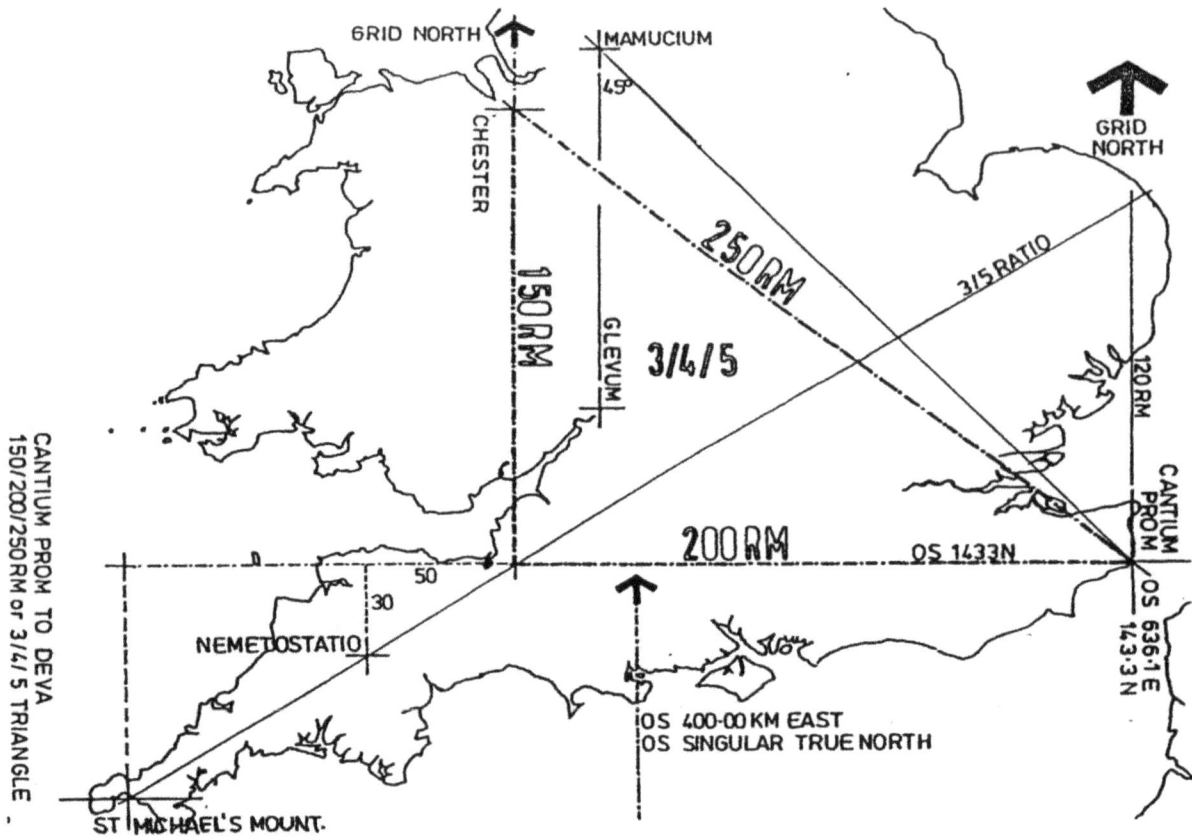

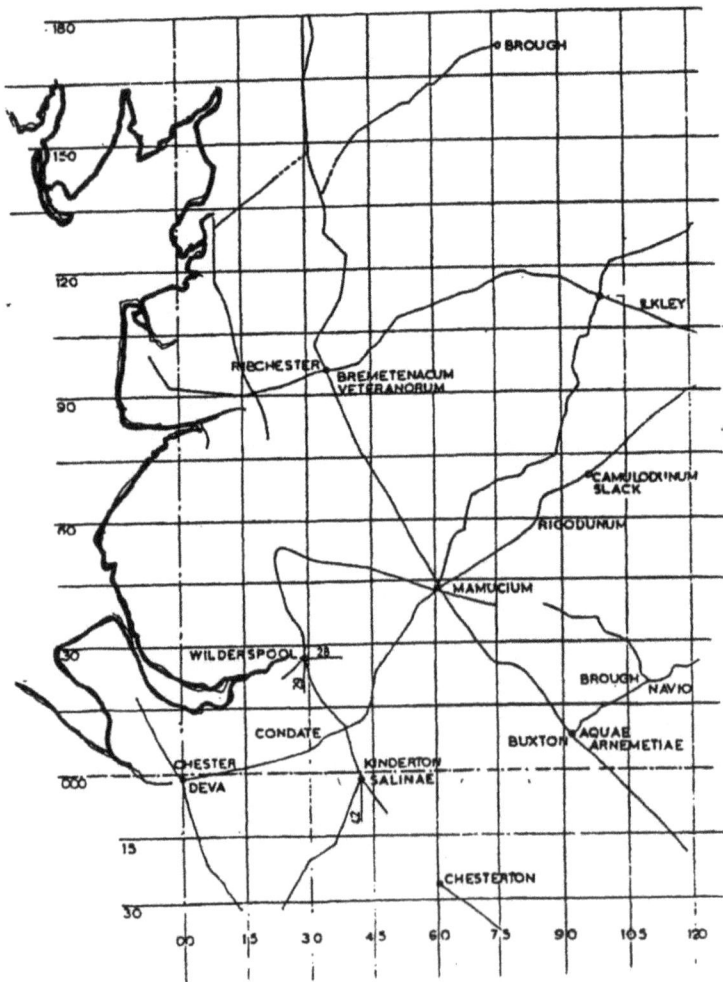

Fig 3.3 (above): **Relationship of *Cantium Prom* to Chester** (including Manchester and Cornwall)

Fig 3.4 (left): **The grid in NW England as measured from Chester**

20

the fortress (OS 365.1N). Now a right-angled triangle is formed between *Cantium Prom*, the Chester datum point and the grid line intersection point at OS 340.60E 143.30N. It is the classic Pythagorean 3:4:5 triangle with the units of 50 Roman miles; 200 being 4 x 50 and 150 being 3 x 150. The hypotenuse connecting *Cantium Prom* to Chester is 250 miles long. See Figure 3.3. It seems that the position of the Chester fortress was chosen with the aid of the map unless its position relative to *Cantium Prom* is a strange co-incidence. It was probably also intended to be as near as possible to the mid latitude of the intended province, if not that of the whole island.

Standing on the mid latitude, Chester may also have been intended as the main survey office. The elliptical building with its monumental proportions and bays, reminiscent of a library, appears suitable for a land registry and survey archive. Sextus Julius Frontinus, author of several texts preserved in the *Corpus Agrimensorum Romanorum*, was the governor active at Chester at the time of the building's inception; but if this was his intention, his plan was abandoned.

The datum point at Wall Knowe, on the same the easting as the Chester fortress, (OS 340.65E) and within a 100 metres of a line 200 miles west of *Cantium Prom*, is 130.0 Roman miles north of the Chester datum at 365.1 N. This suggests that the grid was extended north of Chester, and was that upon which the Inglewood centuriation and the Reagill – Carlisle road were also planned.

More evidence for the grid north of Chester comes from the fact that several forts lie at whole numbers of *centuriae* from Chester; Wilderspool at 29.0 east and 28.0 north; Kinderton at 42.0 east and 1.0 north, and both Manchester and Chesterton at almost 60 *centuriae* east. The fort at Ilkley (OS 411.60E 448.00N) is 100.4 *centuriae* east and 116.8 *centuriae* north of Chester. Given the error of map scale, it is likely the true values are 100 and 117 respectively. We have already shown above that the road leaving it for Adel runs to an alignment node at Coldharbour, Yeadon that is 15.0 *centuriae* E, and 10.0 *centuriae* S of the Ilkley fort. See Figure 3.4. This alignment node is 115.4 *centuriae* E and 106.4 *centuriae* N of Chester. Thus, the road appears to be the hypotenuse of a triangle whose corners occur at *centuriae* intervals north and east of the Chester datum.

The accuracy of the survey
It is now pertinent to comment on the question of survey error since the evidence points to the *agrimensores* having worked to a very high standard. It is, of course, impossible to carry out surveys, or any form of measurement, without some error, but the *groma*, though a simple instrument, could be used to great effect. It had a most significant feature, the arm or bracket, which connected the upright staff to the cross-arms. Fabricius (1901) reconstructed one from the information given in the *Corpus Agrimensorum* and concluded that this arm enabled the axis of the off-set cross-piece to be placed exactly above the datum peg from which the measurements were to be made. Della Corte (1912) discovered at Pompeii several metal fittings that he identified as the furnishings of a *groma* and his reconstructed instrument had an arm 2.5 cm long. This can only mean that such an instrument was intended for land measurements that were accurate at least to the inch. However, Schioler (1994) has denied that *gromae* were furnished with such arms and to support his view cited their absence on two tombstones. The point may therefore be in dispute, but all the evidence, especially that from the Inglewood centuriation and the Carlisle – Reagill road, indicates that Roman surveyors did work to a very accurate standard.

Manpower and surveying effort
A ready objection by those uncomfortable with evidence of Roman surveying ingenuity is that the required effort was quite beyond them. It is a professional surveyor's opinion (MJF) that teams of three men could align 100 *actus* per day in square patterns, that is ten lines of 2.2 miles, covering 4.8 sq. miles. This represents 1.6 sq. miles per man per day. With more men a larger area could be covered in the same time. An area 320 miles wide EW (*Cantium Prom* to St Michael's Mount) and extending 150 miles north of Cantium *Prom*, is 48,000 sq. miles. This area would have needed 30,000 man-days, or 300 days work from 100 men. But much of this area is sea, so the land survey would have required much less effort. It is likely 150 men could have done it in the six warmer months of the year. We would stress that this initial exercise would involve nothing more than placing marker posts and perhaps noting major features; it would not necessarily involve detailed mapping.

Discussion
In summary, we suggest that the first surveying objectives after the invasion were to define an EW base line and establish the mid longitude, just as Claudius Ptolemy was later to recommend. The surveyors probably measured the lines in Roman miles and chose the mid longitude at 160 miles W of *Cantium Prom*. The next phase saw the setting out of secondary survey lines NSEW from the base lines, cross-linking with them to make an orthogonal grid. As the grid was extended across the country, the map would be composed square by square. The Foss Way planning line was then set out across the map grid at *Atan* 3/5 E of N, after the positions of the proposed sites at Leicester and Axminster had been decided upon, though it is almost certain that it was always intended that the two places should fit the line rather than the line connect two previously chosen places. This suggested scheme would account for the very early Roman interest in the Gloucestershire and Wiltshire area (from where the line of mid longitude was driven north. The recent dating of the Alchester fortress to AD 44 (Sauer 2001) supports this contention. The country south of the Chester parallel (the mid latitude) was probably surveyed in the first phase, with that to north in the second.

From this interpretation, it would appear that much of Britain was competently surveyed at least 40 years before Claudius Ptolemy was born by *agrimensores* who were quite accomplished at dealing with the practical problems of mapping. They chose a mid longitude with the same logic as the Ordnance Survey and produced a map which for their purposes was every bit as accurate. It looks as though they worked to Eratosthenes's world model with 75 Roman miles per degree of latitude and solved the problem of map projection by the very device that Claudius Ptolemy gave later. They probably regarded the country south of the Tyne-Solway line as a separate entity from that to north, and the map of Scotland, which is so hopelessly corrupted in the surviving mediaeval texts of Ptolemy's Geography, was probably a separate undertaking. Refer to Figure 2.9.

We suspect therefore that Claudius Ptolemy's didactic tone may hide the fact that in prescribing a 11:20 longitude-latitude ratio for the British map, he was merely drawing on what had already been done. Professor Dilke drew attention to the significance of his use of the past and the future tenses. Ptolemy wrote that that he "*had* maps drawn up" but when being prescriptive, he used the future tense, "We *shall* etc." (Dilke 1987, 190). This is reminiscent of *De Munitionibus Castrorum* in which Hyginus also used the future tense in laying down what should be done to set out a military camp, even though he as good as admitted that he did not know the basics of the task (Richardson 2000).

This interpretation is somewhat dismissive of the reliability of ancient academic geographers, but is entirely consistent with the conclusions of earlier scholars who have noted marked errors and inconsistencies in the ancient geographical literature. "It must be admitted," wrote two such authorities, "that the extent and accuracy of the knowledge displayed in ancient geographic literature is hardly in keeping with the results of actual exploration. Ancient geographic writers are strangely reticent regarding some of the greatest and most fruitful voyages of discovery" (Cary and Warmington 1963, 227). They continue,"Not content with neglecting good information, geographic authors were prone to cherish false reports long after they had been exploded..." This unsurprising attitude was probably due to vanity and academic detachment from the real world of traders and travellers.

****

PART FOUR

PLANNING THE PROVINCE

Geometric relationships of the Foss Way and Stane Street lines

An odd feature of the map of Roman Britain that has long intrigued scholars is the curiously geometric disposition of sites that were presumably developed for economic and politico-strategic reasons. The idea that these cartographic quirks might be deliberate arrangements is quite abhorrent to the modern utilitarian mind, and when such things are forced upon our attention, we are inclined to dismiss them as aberrations and to remember that the major determinants of landscape are geographical, or even geological, in origin.

There is another objection. If on a grid we were to select, at random, a number of points at grid line intersections, we would be bound to place one point in some sort of geometric (right-angled triangular) relationship to the others, for it would be an unavoidable consequence of selecting the intersections. In such a random selection there would be a wide range of possible angular relationships. But when we come to examine those of many sites in Roman Britain we find certain angles occur frequently. We have already seen *Atan* 3/5 with the Foss Way, Stane Street, the Ribchester to Slaidburn road and the Inglewood centuriation, not forgetting its almost certain occurrence at Florence.

There are several other curiously similar examples. Probably the most obvious is the triangle formed by lines connecting Ilchester, Leicester and Colchester. Between Ilchester and Leicester, the Foss Way marks one side of this triangle. At Leicester a road left the Foss Way at right angles on a line pointing to Colchester but it did not apparently reach that town, though it may have been intended to do so. On a small-scale map it is demonstrable that the right-angled triangle has sides in the ratio 3:4:5. Careful observation on the larger scale map enables this triangle to be defined more accurately and reveals the probable locations of its points. They are all within a mile or so of the centres of the respective towns; Ilchester (352.00E 122.45N), Leicester (461.59E 305.01N), Colchester (598.57E 222.90N). The distances between the points are: Ilchester to Leicester, 144.0 miles (300.0 *centuriae*): Leicester to Colchester, 108 miles (225 *centuriae*): Colchester to Ilchester 180 miles (375 *centuriae*). The unitary dimension of this triangle is 75 *centuriae*, or 36 Roman miles: that is, 225/3 = 300/4 = 375/5 = 75. It is significant that this dimension is common to military and agrimensorial measure.

However, when the 300 *centuriae* Ilchester to Leicester line is projected to 400 *centuriae*, it terminates at a point very near the Foss Way alignment node south of Lincoln cathedral, actually at 498.12E 365.98N. This 400-*centuriae* line (192, or 16 x 12, Roman miles) now forms the hypotenuse of another right-angled triangle (sides in the ratio 3:5) relating Lincoln to Ilchester along the NS and EW grid lines. The other sides are 205.8 *centuriae* EW and 343 *centuriae* NS; 98.78 and 164.6 Roman miles respectively. So while the *lengths* of the two mean Foss Way lines are whole numbers of *centuriae* and miles, those along the relevant NSEW grid lines are not. See Figure 4.1.

A similar situation is seen with Stane Street whose geometry was described in Part 2. Converting the distances given in that section to Roman measure, we have:

	EW	NS	Hypotenuse i.e. road line
Km	46.4	75.5	88.6
Miles	31.4	51.1	59.9
Centuriae	65.4	106.4	124.9

Thus the alignment dimension (hypotenuse) is almost certainly in whole numbers of Roman measure, 60 miles (125 *centuriae*,) unlike the EW distance, 31.4 miles (65.4 *centuriae*). The NS distance is 51.1 miles, arguably 51, or 106.36 *centuria*.

These observations suggest that the distances, between towns, as the crow flies, were intended to be hypotenuses in *whole number* units, but were drafted upon a NSEW grid such that the non-hypotenuse sides were *not* whole number units. This is a most curious situation and suggests that a grid aligned at the same angle as the hypotenuses, namely, *Atan* 3/5, was actually used to *plan* the distribution of the towns and thus define the lines of the interconnecting roads. If this supposition is correct, there should be further corroborative evidence.

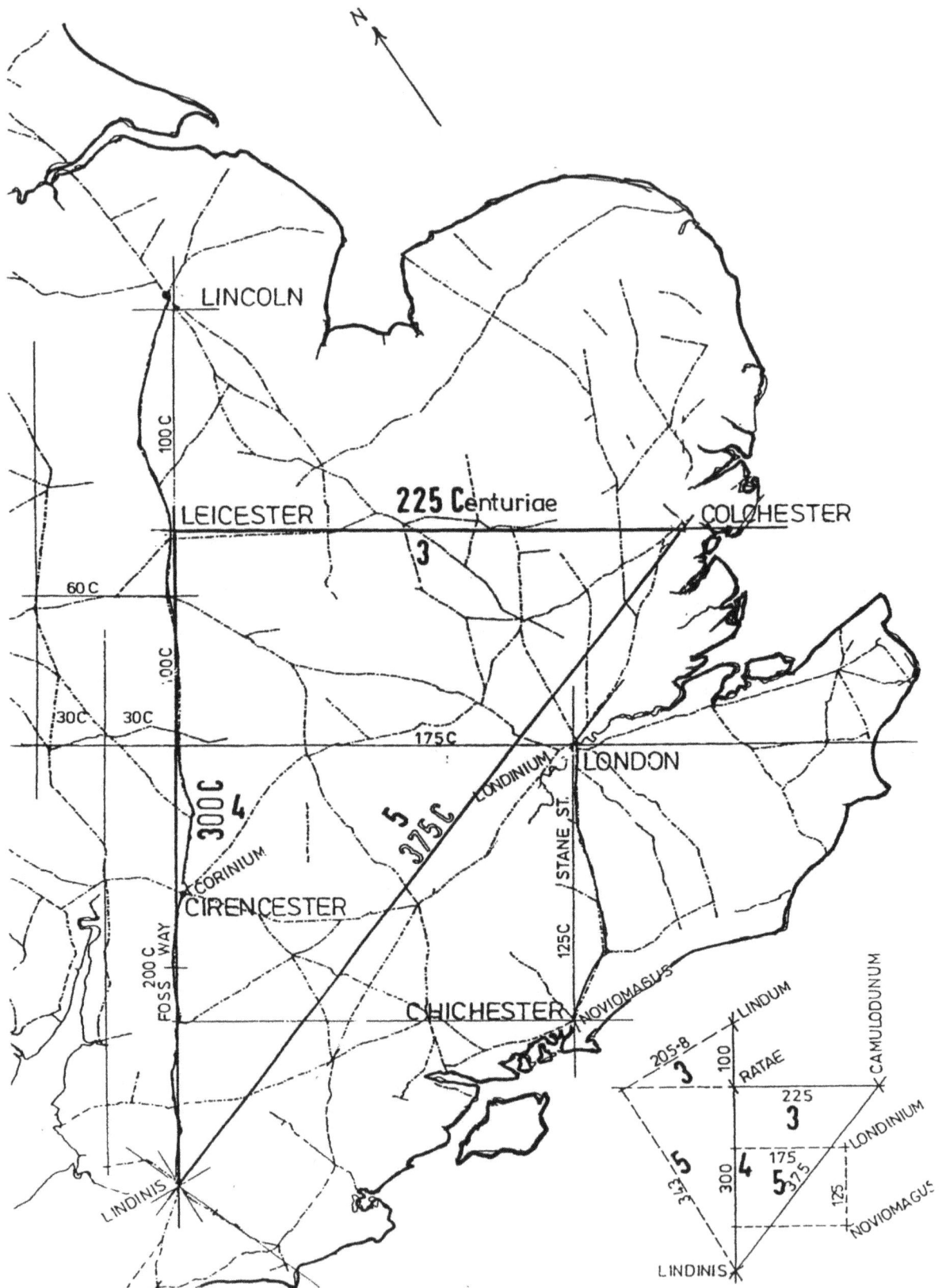

Fig 4.1
The Foss Way and Stane Street
(They are parallel and separated by 175 *centuriae*)

The planning grid of the province

A grid angled *Atan* 3/5 E of N, with an origin at the *Cantium Prom* datum point, can be superimposed on the map of Roman of Roman Britain. When its lines are marked at intervals of 60 *centuriae*, they fit readily with a surprisingly large number of roads and towns across the whole country. Figure 4.2 shows such a map south of the Clyde-Forth line. In some places the squares are bisected to show the 30-*centuriae* lines and it is difficult to resist the conclusion that the road network harmonises with this grid. Moreover, south of the Humber-Mersey line, the Foss Way and the Stane Street follow parallel grid lines 175 *centuriae* apart, the former at 330 *centuriae,* and the latter close to (less than 5 *centuriae*) 150 *centuriae,* from a parallel line through *Cantium Prom.*

North of the Humber-Mersey line, however, this grid inclination does not harmonise with the lie of the land, which bends northwest. The road network now better fits a grid aligned *Atan* 3/5 W of N. See Figure 4.3. Dere Street in the Vale of York runs very close to a line from *Cantium Prom* through Lincoln, and the Reagill-Carlisle road, which we have demonstrated aligns *Atan* ½ W of N, approximates *Atan* 3/5 W of N. This is not a contradiction, merely an effect of scale, the difference being only 4.4 ° and therefore insignificant on a high scale map.

When these two grids are superimposed upon the NSEW grid, (Figures 4.4 and 4.10) they account for much of the Roman road network, and Watling Street from London to Wroxeter best shows how the two overlapping grids appear to have been used. From London to north of *Verulamium*, Watling Street approximates the 3/5 W of N grid line 120 *centuriae* from *Cantium Prom*. Then it approximates the other grid (N of W) to *Lactodorum*, and then switches back to the first grid until High Cross where it reverts again to the second grid as far as Wall. From there to Wroxeter it approximates to the NSEW grid by following a more or less EW line. These are approximations since throughout the route's length the actual causeway sub-alignments are defined by other angles relative to the NSEW grid.

This is also seen with the Chester to York route and its extensions to the Welsh and Yorkshire coasts at Barmouth and Flamborough Head. See Figure 4.5. The whole route closely approximates a line inclined *Atan* 3/5 N of E at 480 *centuriae* from *Cantium Prom* but the sub-alignments relate to the NSEW grid. Table 4.1 shows the details of the alignment between the Chester and York fortresses and the OS grid references of the alignment nodes are listed in Appendix 9. York lies *Atan* 7/10 N of E from Chester with this clearly defines the mean line of the route. But the actual causeway pursues that angle only between Manchester and Castle Shaw. Note that east of Tadcaster Bridge, as the road approaches York, the remaining alignment nodes are again *Atan* 7/10 N of E from Chester.

The grid, angled *Atan* 3/5 W of N also describes the disposition of twelve Roman towns in the West Country. Figure 4.6 shows them lying within the rough triangle formed between Gloucester, Ilchester and the Isle of Wight; the intervening distances were determined by trigonometry from their OS grid references (1:25,000 maps). Within the triangle, three smaller triangles are formed by the following towns: a) *Glevum, Corinium, Cunetio*: b) *Cunetio, Calleva, Venta*: c) *Venta, Noviomagus, Vectis* (Carisbrooke). The mean intervening distance is 60.0 *centuriae*. See Table 4.2. *Corinium* and the Foss Way's mean line are 330 *centuriae* W of *Cantium Prom*; see above. *Corinium* is at the apex of an isosceles triangle whose two equal sides are formed by the Foss Way's line and that of the *Corinium - Venta* route. See Figure 4.7. It seems that in this part of the country Roman planning required towns to be arranged in a triangular matrix of 60-*centuriae* dimensions, aligned according to the angled grid. The plan was not, of course, perversely and stubbornly imprinted upon the landscape in defiance of topography and economics, but the overall concept is plain to see.

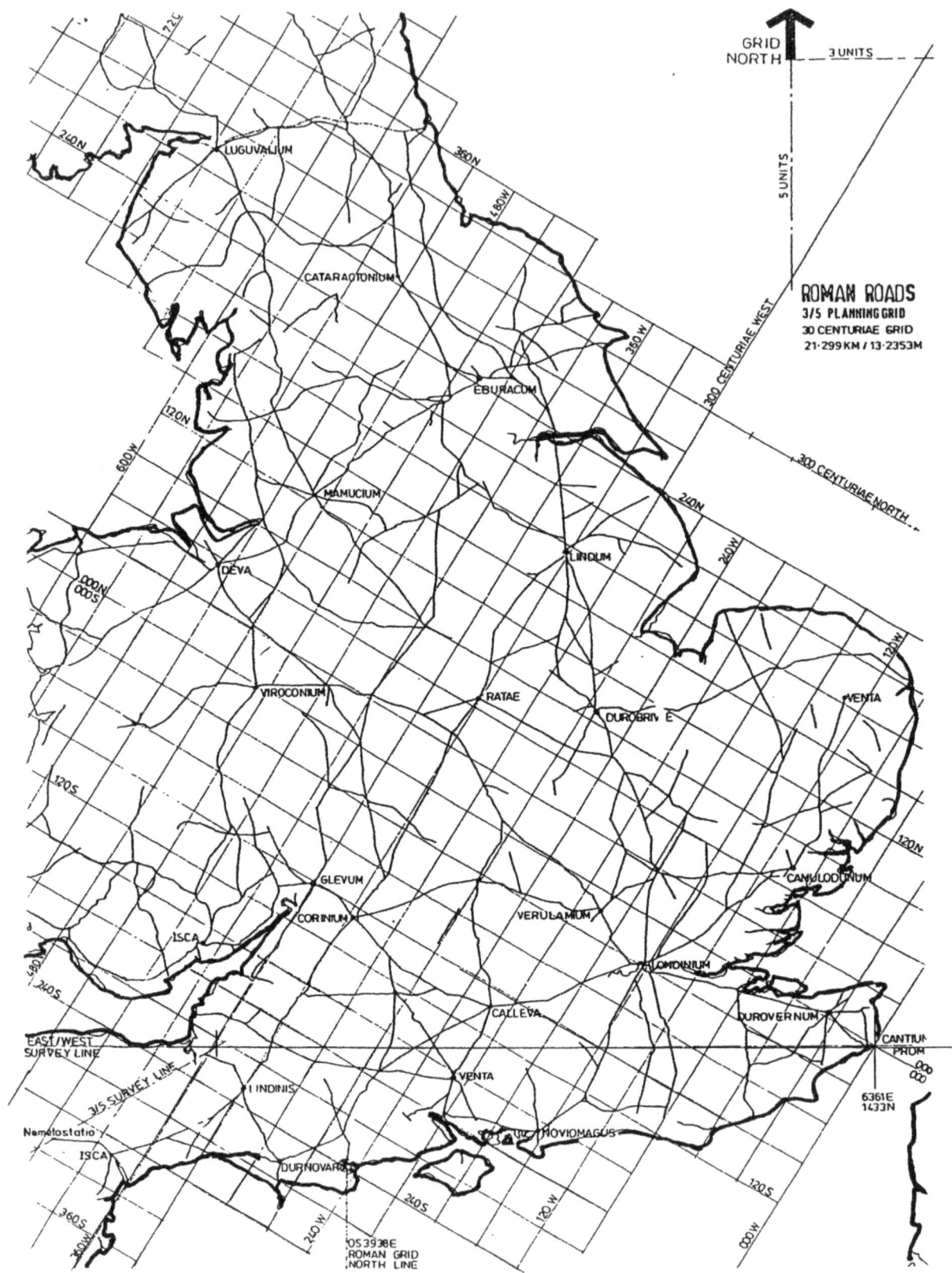

Fig 4.2
Planning grid inclined *Atan* 3/5 E of N
(Grid lines at 30 *centuriae* intervals: Note roads parallel to grid lines)

26

COLONIAE
CANTONAL CAPITALS
WALLED TOWNS
3/5 PLANNING GRID
30 CENTURIAE GRID
21·299 KM / 13·2353M

NORTH

3 UNITS

5 UNITS
GRID NORTH
AT OS 3938E

600 N

480 N

360 N

240 N

120 N

000

120 E

600 E
000

120 W

240 W

480 N

360 N

240 N

120 W

240 W

360 N

000 N

120 W

LUGUVALIUM

CATARACTONIUM

ISURIUM

EBURACUM

PETUARIA

MAMUCIUM

AQUAE ARNEMETIAE

DEVA

MARGIDUNUM

LINDUM

CAUSENNAE

VIROCONIUM

LETOCETUM

RATAE

DUROBRIVAE

VENTA

SALINAE

IRCHESTER

DUROLIPONS

LACTODORUM

C C

MAGNIS

ALCHESTER

CAMULODUNUM

GLEVUM

B

CORINIUM

VERULAMIUM

D

LONDINIUM

AQUAE SULIS

CUNETIO

CALLEVA

DUROBRIVAE

DUROVERNUM

EAST/WEST
SURVEY LINE

CANTIUM PROM.
OS 6361E
1433N

3/5 SURVEY LINE

VENTA

LINDINIS

OS 6036N

ISCA

CLAUSENTUM

NOVIOMAGUS

DURNOVARIA

OS 3938E
ROMAN GRID
NORTH LINE

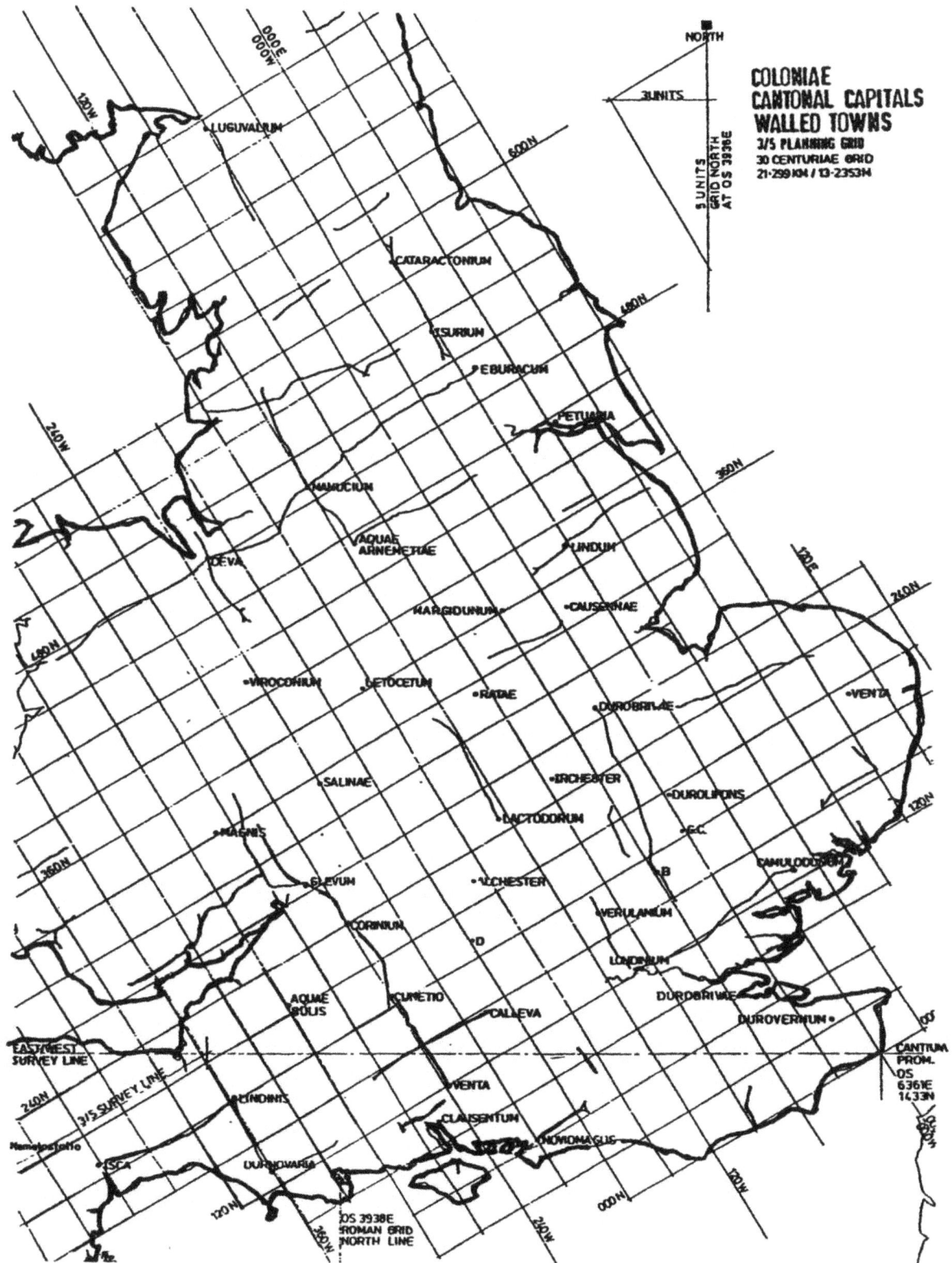

Fig 4.3
Planning grid inclined *Atan* 3/5 W of N
(Grid lines at 30 *centuriae* intervals Note roads parallel to grid lines)

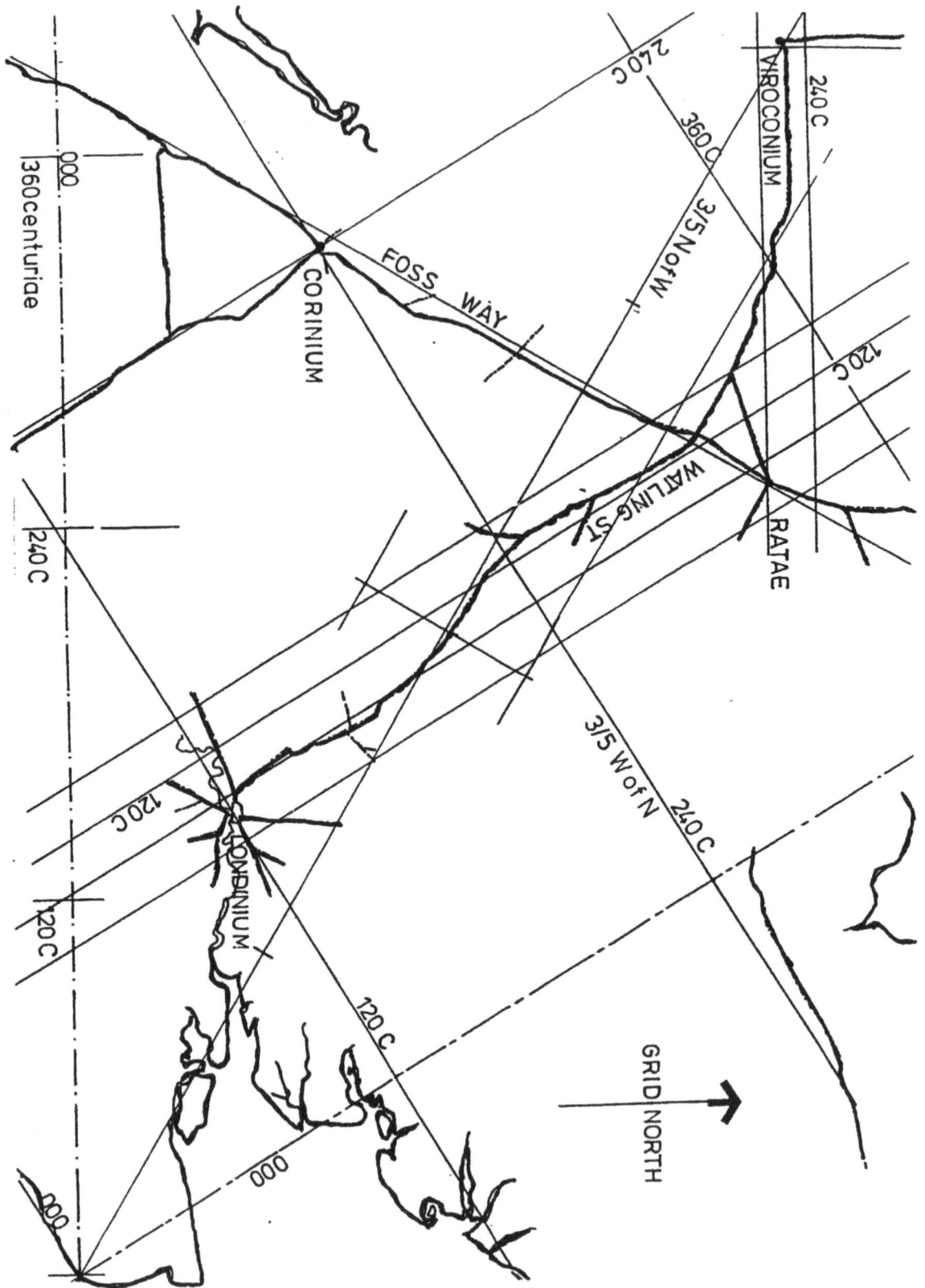

Fig 4.4
Watling Street (A5) in relation to *Atan 3/5* planning grids
(Grid lines are W of N, N of W and E of N)

Labels on figure: VIROCONIUM, CORINIUM, RATAE, FOSS WAY, WATLING ST, LONDINIUM, 360centuriae, GRID NORTH

Grid values: 240 C, 360 C, 120 C, 3/5 N of W, 3/5 W of N, 000

Table 4.1
Alignment inclination (N of E) of road sections between Chester and York

Angles are expressed as the decimal tangent and the rational fraction

Point	Section alignment		Alignment from Chester	
Chester cathedral				
Eddisbury	(0.19)	1/5	(0.19)	1/5
Northwich Bridge	(0.42)	2/5	(0.28)	)
King Street junction	(0.38)	2/5	(0.29)	) mean 3/10
Holford Farm	(0.47)	1/2	(0.31)	)
Tabley House	(1.7)	8/5 ?	(0.37)	2/5
Bucklow Hill Nth	(5.13)	5/1 ?	(0.54)	1/2
Crossford Bridge	(1.54)	3/2	(0.69)	7/10
Stretford	(2.21)	11/10	(0.74)	3/4
Manchester fort	(0.67)	7/10 ?	(0.73)	3/4
Castle Shaw	(0.72)	7/10 ?	(0.73)	3/4
Outlane Slack	(0.90)	9/10	(0.75)	3/4
Holme Farm	(0.84)	2/5	(0.78)	3/4 to 2/5 ?
Hope Hall	(0.20)	1/5	(0.76)	3/4
Tadcaster Bridge	(0.09)	1/10	(0.71)	7/10
Hagg Wood	(0.46)	1/2	(0.70)	7/10
Bond Hill	(0.52)	1/2	(0.69)	7/10
York Minster	(2.39)	12/10	(0.71)	7/10

Table 4.2
Direct line distances in *centuriae* between certain Roman sites

	From	To	Distance	Means
Triangle A				
	Corinium	*Cunetio*	52.8	
	Cunetio	*Aquae Sulis*	64.6	
	Aquae Sulis	*Corinium*	64.4	60.6
Triangle B				
	Cunetio	*Calleva*	59.7	
	Calleva	*Venta*	50.4	
	Venta	*Cunetio*	68.4	59.5
Triangle C				
	Venta	*Noviomagus*	63.4	
	Noviomagus	*Vectis*	57.9	
	Vectis	*Venta*	58.5	60.0

Dimensional units used with the planning grid

When the geometric inter-relationships of certain other Roman sites are determined some curious triangular patterns emerge, with equally curious dimensions.

First consider the 3:5 right-angled triangle. From the Pythagorean theorem, the unitary dimension of its hypotenuse is sq. root of (9 + 25 = 34) or 5.83. This means that when the other sides are integers (whole numbers) the hypotenuse is fractional. When, however, the hypotenuse is an integer, the other sides are fractional. For example, if the hypotenuse is 100 units, then the unitary dimension is 100 / 5.83 = 17.15 and the other sides are 17.15 x 3 = 51.45 and 17.15 x 5 = 85.76. There is evidence in the Roman map of Britain of 3:5 triangles with hypotenuses of both fractional and integer values and whose other sides, aligning on the NSEW grid, have corresponding integer and fractional values.

Fig 4.5 Barmouth – Flamborough : Atan 3/5 N of E and 480 *centuriae* from *Cantium Prom*

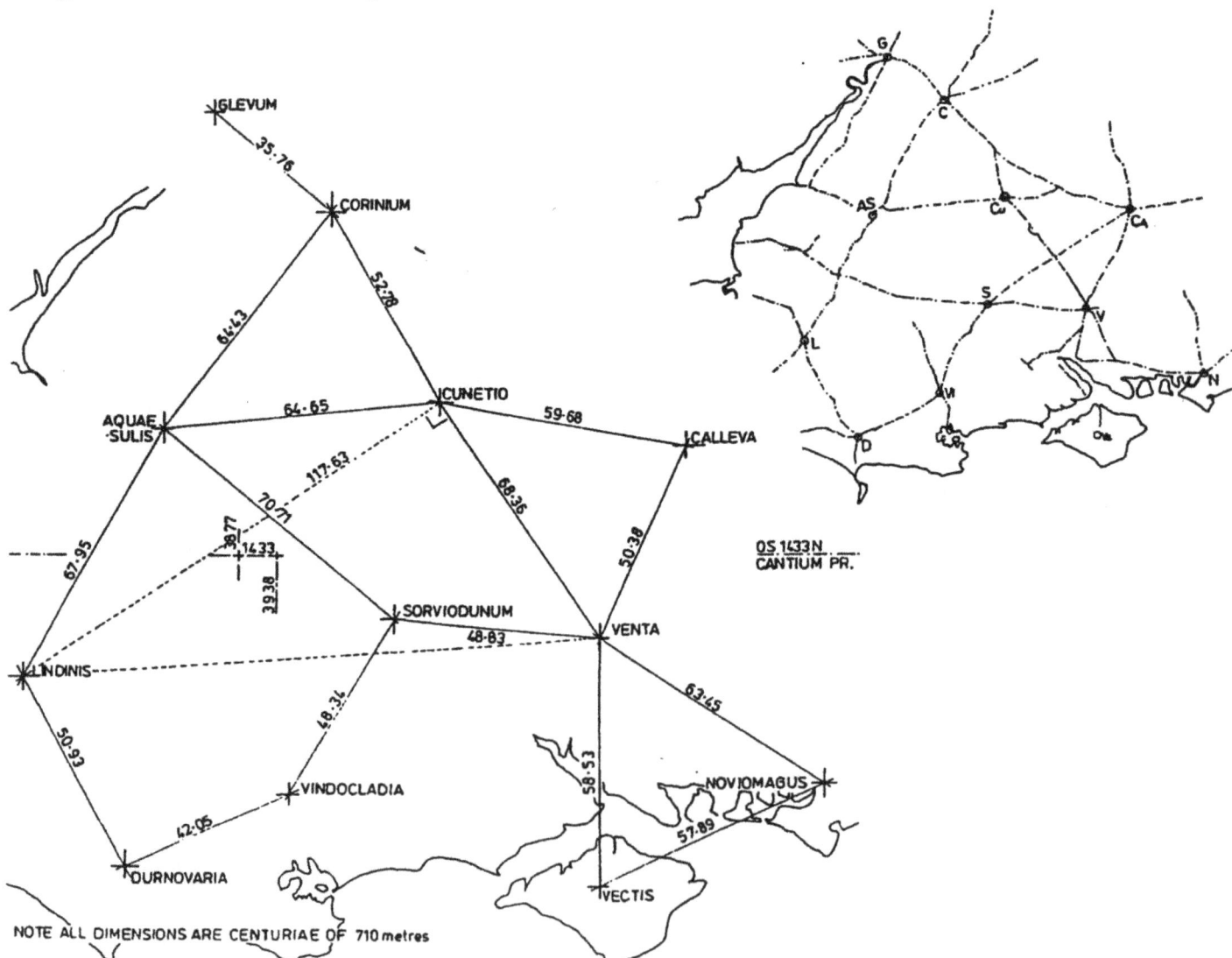

NOTE ALL DIMENSIONS ARE CENTURIAE OF 710 metres

Fig 4.6 Spacing of twelve Roman towns in the West Country

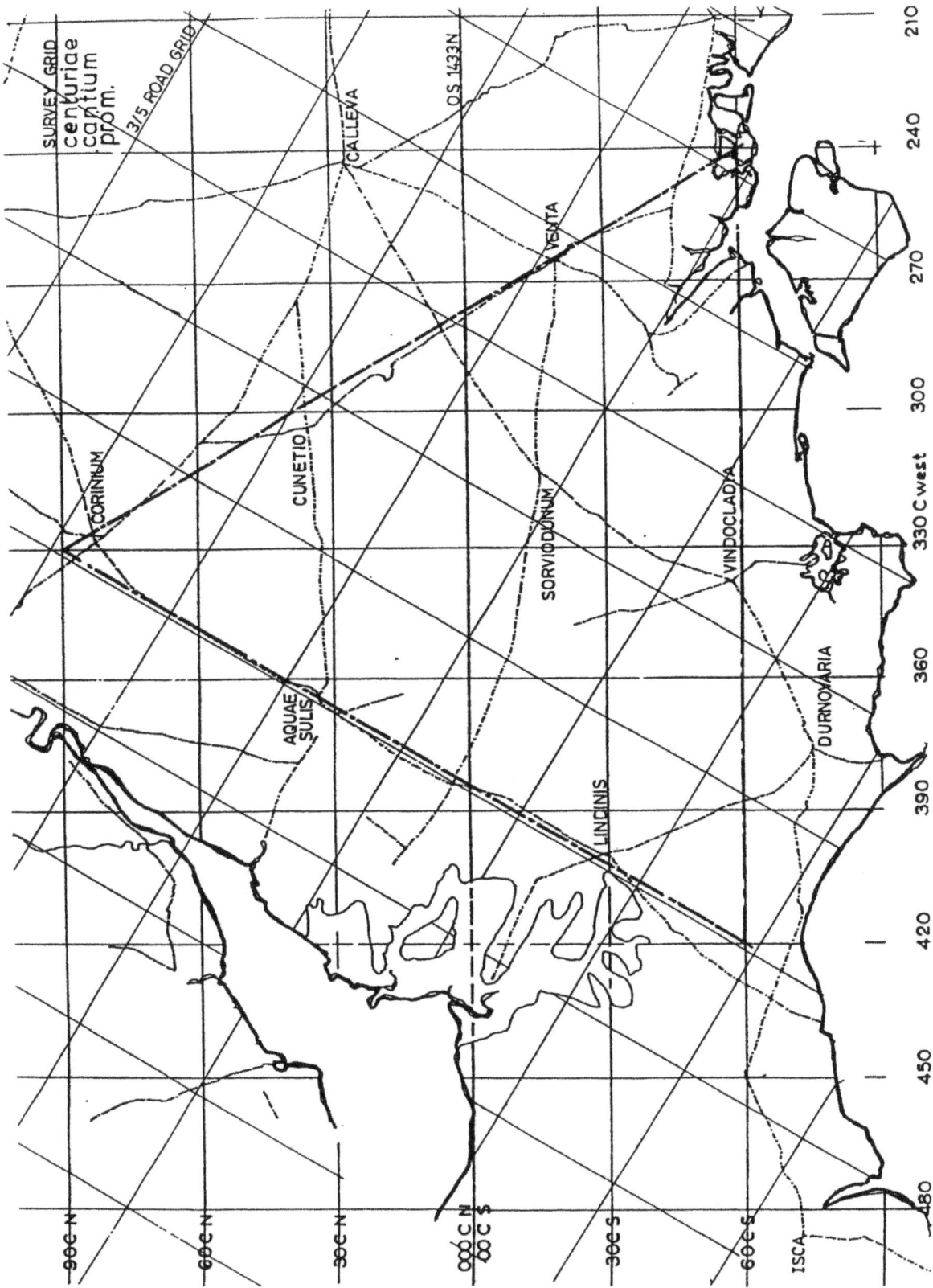

Fig. 4.7 Planning in the West Country
(The triangle is aligned on OS grid NSEW)

Hypotenuse with a fractional value: A line from the intersection of the *Cantium Prom* parallel and the Wall Knowe-Chester meridian (OS 340.60E 143.30N) to St Michael's Mount forms the hypotenuse of a 3:5 right-angled triangle. Thirty miles south, and 50 miles west, from the intersection (note the numbers) stands a Roman fort at *Nemetostatio*, (OS 266.10E 0.99.9N). The distances are in the precise proportion in miles. When the hypotenuse *Atan* 3/5 N of E from St Michael's Mount to *Nemetostatio* is projected, it meets a line due north from *Cantium Prom* to form the hypotenuse of another right-angled triangle with sides in the ratio 3:5. These are 120 and 200 miles long, so their unitary dimension is 40 miles, with the hypotenuse 5.83 x 40 = 233.2 miles. See Figure 4.8.

Hypotenuses with integer values: If a hypotenuse were 100 miles long, its unitary dimension would be 100 / 5.83 = 17.15 miles (see above). This value, can be detected in the Roman map. Gloucester (OS 383.18E) and Manchester (OS 383.20E) occur on virtually the same easting at 17.15 x 10 = 171.5 miles east of *Cantium Prom*. Manchester is the same distance north. It therefore bears 45° W of N from *Cantium Prom* and the line joining them is the diagonal of a square. Gloucester, (224.53N) is 17.15 x 3 = 51.45 miles north of *Cantium Prom*. So the Manchester – *Cantium Prom* line is also the hypotenuse of an isosceles triangle. See Figure 4.8.

York is very close to a line *Atan* 3/5 W of N from *Cantium Prom*. It is virtually 208.8 (17.15 x 12) miles north of that place and 120 (17.15 x 7) miles east. But the direct line, the hypotenuse, is 240 (17.15 x 14) miles. The latter value is an integer. A line running SW from York at 45° meets the parallel of *Cantium Prom* at the meridian of St Michael's Mount There can be little doubt that York stands in geometric relationship to *Cantium Prom*. See Figure 4.9. Whether this was intentional or merely a consequence of using a grid for planning is problematical.

The significance of the angled planning grid and dimensional units

A reasonable interpretation of these findings is that the unitary dimensional values of the hypotenuses of the 3 by 4 triangle (5) and the 3 by 5 triangle (5.83) and their squares, 25 and 34, were regarded as desirable dimensions using an angled planning grid. What are the likely reasons for such a peculiar approach to town and country planning?

Orientation of Britain: One reason almost certainly lies in Britain's physical geography. The east coast broadly inclines *Atan* 3/5 W of N and the ridges and vales of the English midlands, tend to run broadly NE – SW. A grid aligned NSEW therefore tends cut across the grain of the country with practical implications for Roman surveyors, for measurements would be more accurately made along the vistas of the obliquely running ridges and vales than across the face of the slopes. A NSEW grid could be set out easily from such a line by triangulation because the hypotenuse on the 3/5 right-angled triangle conveniently relates by simple Roman measures to an orthogonal agrimensorial grid.

Consider, for example, a long line laid out *Atan* 3/5 E of N, over open ground after determining the direction of north from solar observation. This line can be made the hypotenuse to triangles whose other sides would lie on NS and EW lines. At every 5.83 unit interval a new NSEW grid line intersection; 3 units E and 5 units N. If measured in *actus*, the units of 3, 5 and 5.83 translate to 360 feet, 600 feet and 699.6, which is only five inches short of 700 feet; easy to remember and easy to lay out. Table 4.3 indicates how multiples of *actus* interrelate.

Table 4.3
Dimensions in feet of the sides of a 3:5 right-angled triangle

unit	EW	NS	Hypotenuse	
actus	360	600	699.6	6 inches short of 700 feet
2 *actus* unit	720	1,200	1,399.4	8 inches short of 1,400 feet
centuriae	2,400	4,000	13,992	8 feet short of 14,000 feet

The points corresponding to whole numbers of *actus* on the NSEW grid could be marked at intervals along the line, as shown in Table 4.4.

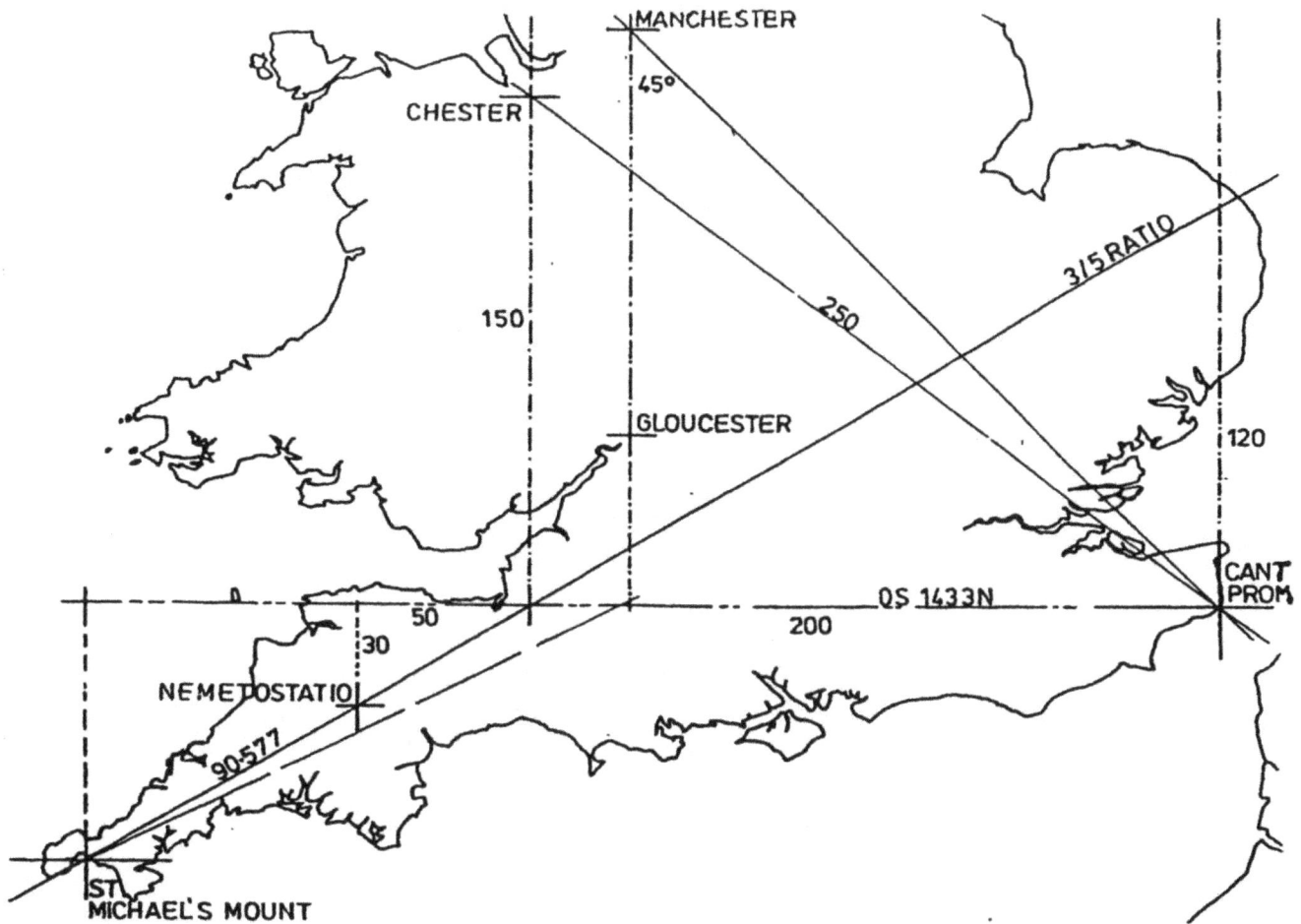

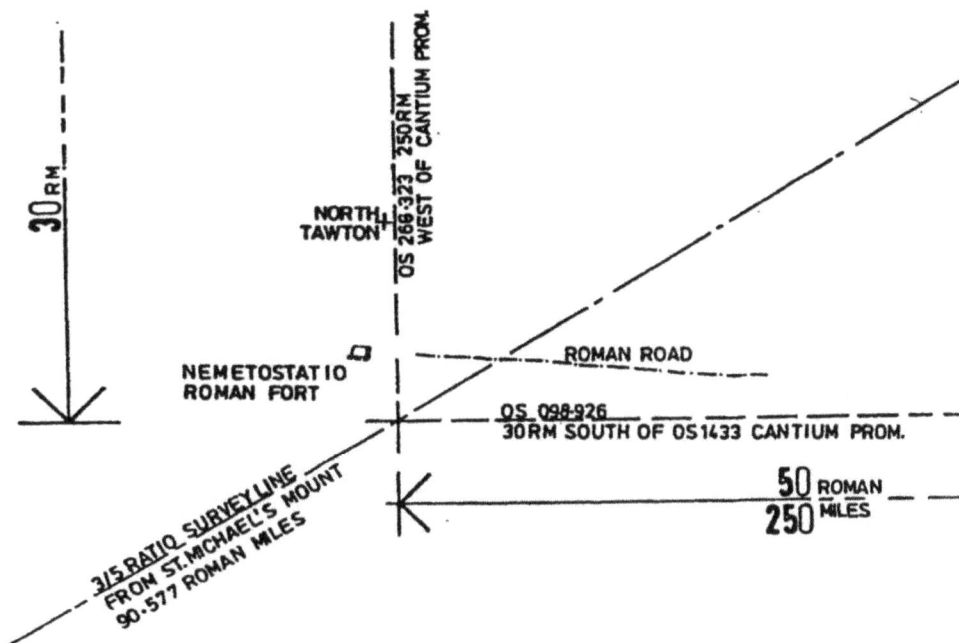

Fig. 4.8 Cornwall: Suggested survey lines and marker station
(Note relationship of Chester, Manchester and Gloucester to *Cantium Prom*)

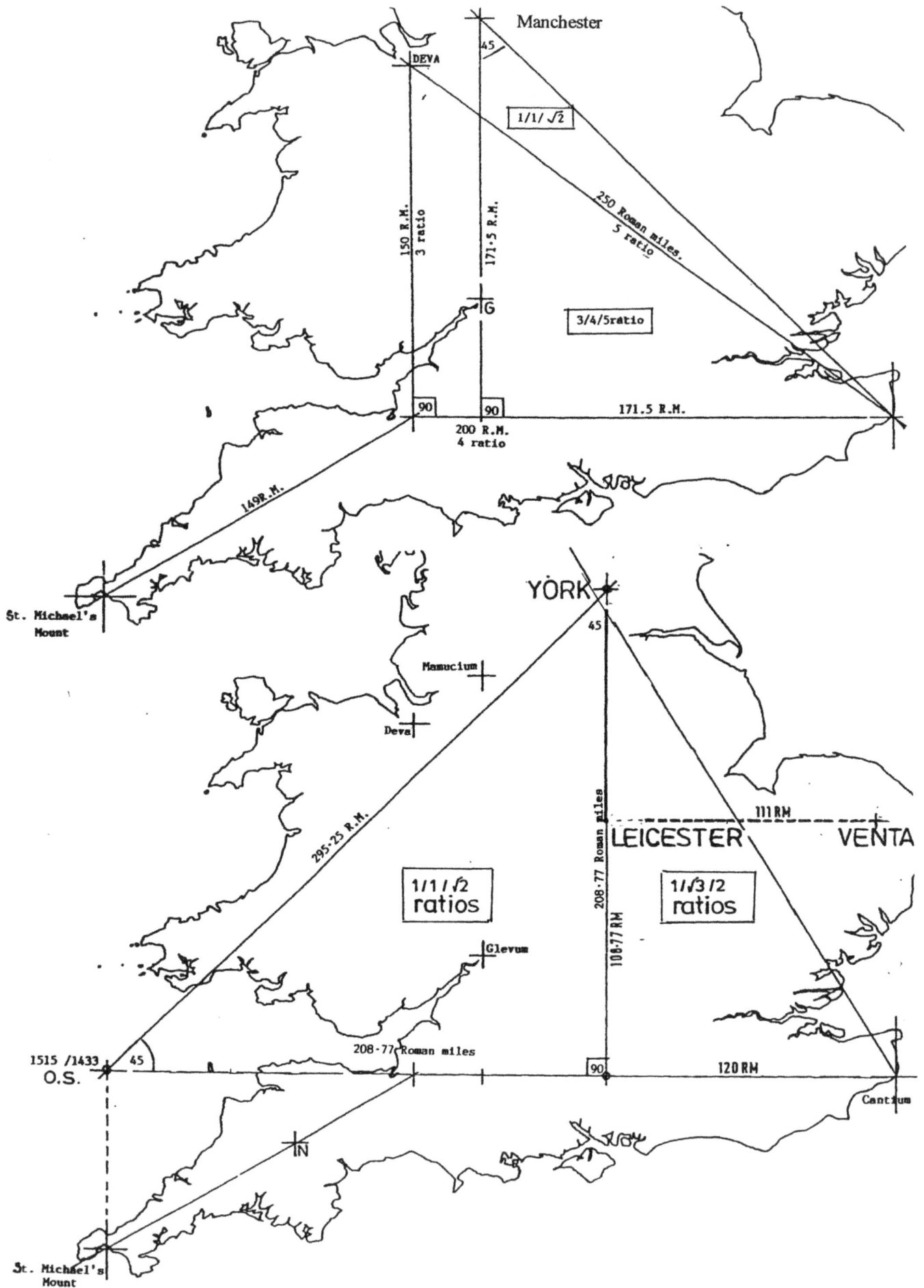

Fig 4.9   Triangle ratios related to *Cantium Prom*
(Above; Chester & Manchester: Below; York)

34

Table 4.4
Actus **units on an orthogonal grid related to those on the hypotenuse**

Intervals in feet along the hypotenuse	EW		NS	
70	36		60	(1/2 *actus*)
140	72		120	(1 *actus*)
1399.4 5 ins short of 1,400 ft.	720	(6 *actus*)	1,200	(10 *actus*)
13,994.25, 5 ft 9 ins short of 14,000 ft.	7,200	(60 *actus*)	12,000	(100 *actus*)

Britain within the world model of Eratosthenes: Another possible reason for the frequency of the angle *Atan* 3/5 in Roman Britain is the *Cosine* rule for the latitude to longitude ratio. At 53° N the *Cosine* is 0.6, or 3/5. On Ptolemy's map, which we must never forget was drawn some 100 years after the survey of Britain, the 53° N line ran along the south coast between Beachy Head and Portsmouth and was thus one degree below that of *Cantium Prom* at 54° N where the *Cosine* was 0.59, almost the same. It is at least possible that the *Cosine* rule influenced the choice of the 3:5 ratio for planning the province's infrastructure. It is certainly a curious coincidence that the very ratio that fits well with Britain's physical geography is that derived from the *Cosine* rule for the only portion of the south coast that runs due EW. Ptolemy did not prescribe a 3/5 ratio for the British map, but one of 11/20, or 0.55 because he adjusted Britain's mid latitude to 56.63° N, almost certainly as a result of having seen the maps that the Roman surveyors of Britain had provided. See Figure 4.10.

Chester, as we have seen, is two degrees (Eratosthenes) north of *Cantium Prom*, and therefore three degrees north of the Beachy Head parallel See Figure 4.11. If it were the parallel chosen for the mid latitude for the province, this would put the map's northern limit at 3 x 75 = 225 miles north of Chester at OS 697.80N. This is 89.6; say 90, miles north of the mean line of Hadrian's Wall, and 15 miles north of the Antonine Wall. It is the parallel that defines the southern edge of the Highland massif in the centre of the Forth – Clyde gap.

The religious dimension: There is a third and probably more fundamental reason for the frequency of both the 3/5 triangle and a planning dimension that is derived from the square on its hypotenuse, and it is entirely consistent with the two aforementioned reasons. It derives from the religious nature of surveying, something that the modern, utilitarian mind does not easily grasp. We see an immediate conflict between being practical and following the dictates of a superstition. To the ancient view, especially the Pythagorean, this was not so. Following a hallowed numerical formula was the best way to guarantee success because it invoked divine protection for the finished work. There is no doubt that surveying and road making were quasi-religious undertakings. For example, an inscription of AD 191, from Brompton on Swale, Yorkshire, makes this clear, *Deo qui vias et samitas commentus est*, "To the god who devised roads and paths". (RIB 275). The Roman army also organised its cavalry and infantry in certain ratios, and its camps and forts were designed with a similar respect for certain proportions, probably in deference to Pythagorean principles (Richardson 2001).

To the Pythagoreans, "The fundamental realities of the world are structural and mathematical." (Anon 1986, 45). "Aristotle," states another authority, " reports that for the Pythagoreans all things are numbers or imitate numbers…it is by number and proportion that *the world becomes organised and knowable*," (Anon 1996, 1284). Certain numbers were associated with particular attributes; thus *one* was male, and *two* was female, an unreliable duality; *three* was marriage, or perhaps harmony (Burn 1965, 138-139). The triangle, having three sides and three angles, seems to have been the geometric figure that best expressed this notion. There is plenty of evidence that the cult of the triangle derived from the Pythagoreans was deeply ingrained in Graeco-Roman thinking and persisted into the Christian doctrine of the Trinity even after the Church had eradicated its pagan origins (Evans 1990, 1121). For pagan it certainly was, "…the doctrine cannot be established on scriptural evidence," writes a religious authority (Anon 1987, 54). It probably entered Christian theology through the efforts of people like Severus's wife, Julia Domna, who attempted to fuse Pythagorean principles with Christian tenets to form a new cult around Apollonius of Tyana (De Burgh, 1924, 280). In such cases, mystical geometric notions must have influenced the theological brews that agitated the minds of the time. Certainly, a triangular halo was the early representation of the Trinity in Christian art (Hall 1974, 308-309).

We do not know how Pythagorean philosophy exerted its effect at a practical level in surveying and landscape planning but in general the Pythagoreans were very superstitious and hedged about by taboos (Burn 1965, 138-139). This probably affected their way of working and the triangular shape of Britain and its inclination probably suggested that a 3 by 5 triangle was that proportion most agreeable to the deity who had shaped the land. The fact that the *Cosine* of the intended province's EW base latitude also equalled, or approximated, 3/5 may have signalled what the presiding god, or gods, required. Taking the auspices was an important aspect of Roman surveying and just as it was essential to invoke divine approval by observing the messages written into the innards of sacrificial animals, it was perhaps equally important that towns and road alignments, where possible should be disposed in agreeable triangles. Thus, geometrical arrangements and numerical coincidences in the map, especially

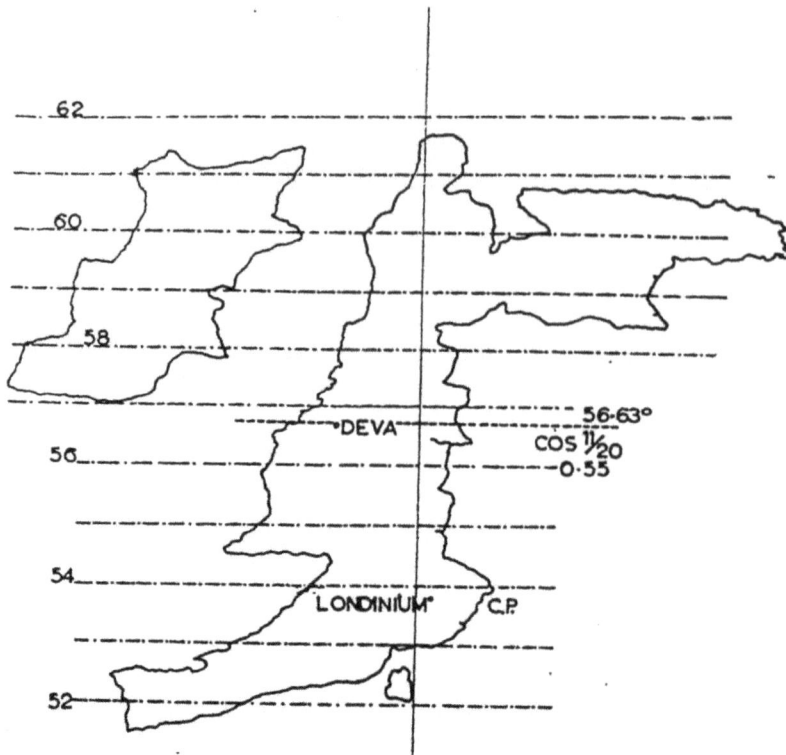

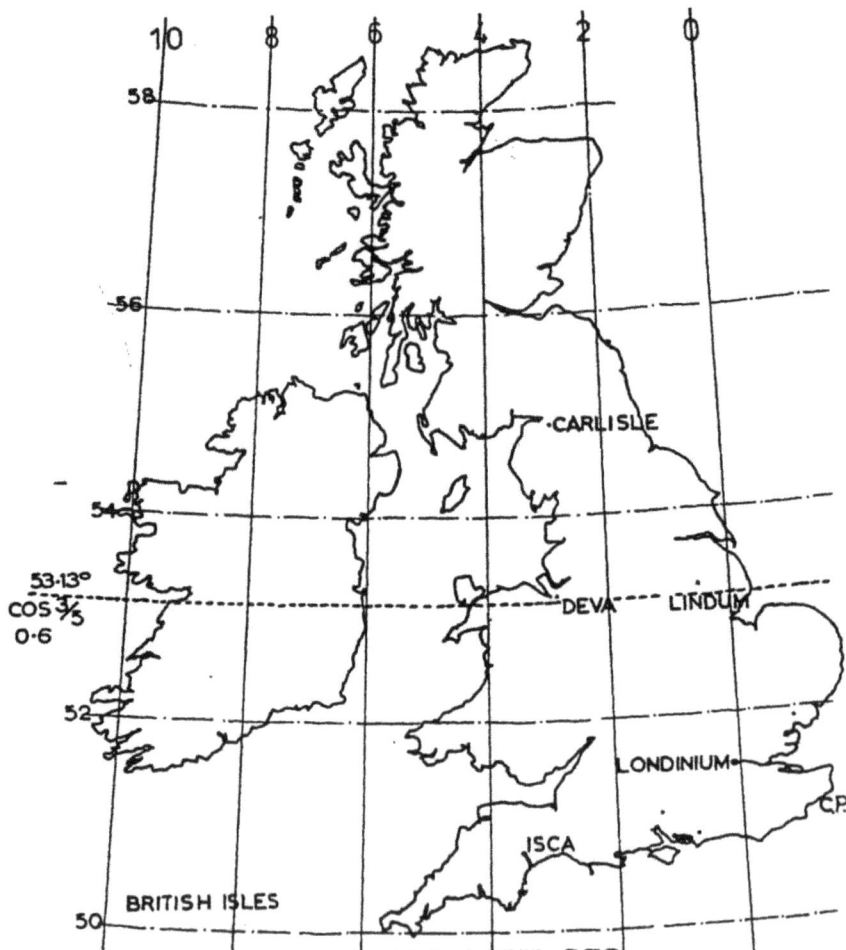

Fig 4.10 Latitude & Longitude
(Above; Ptolemy's latitudes shown on the undoubtedly corrupted version of his map of Britannia)
(Below; Modern latitudes and longitudes; note 2 degree W in OS grid mid latitude)

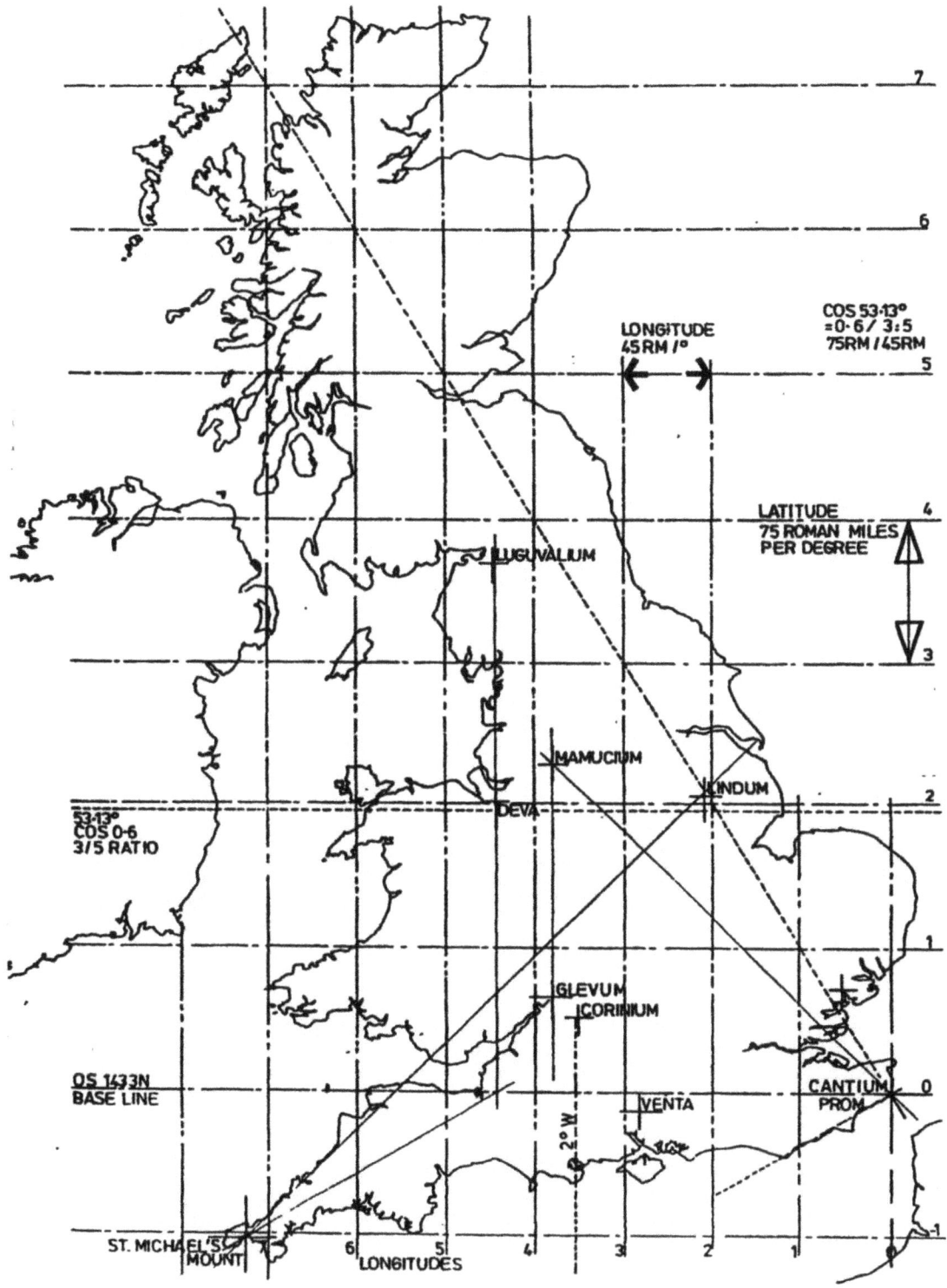

Fig 4.11 The Modern map with latitudes and longitudes marked in the proportion of the putative Roman model

37

dimensions that are squares and sq. roots of standard hypotenuse lengths, should not be dismissed out of hand. Almost certainly Roman engineers preferred to work in harmony with the landscape rather than offend the gods by brashly conquering it, as would have a Victorian. In the Far East such concerns still hold sway and buildings and towns are not sited without regard to similar ancient superstitions, termed *geomancy*.* The aligning of churches along an EW line is probably the only remnant of this ancient way of working to have survived in the West; but it shows how such things were once regarded. So when we detect surprising triangular relationships on the Roman map, we are not deluding ourselves by making patterns that are not there, nor seeing a perverse addiction to nonsense by Roman planners; we are detecting evidence of their religious scruples. See Appendices 12 and 13.

****

PART FIVE

CENTURIATION

In Part 2 we referred to the angles of alignment of *limites* in some centurial systems in Britain. Some of these systems are worth further consideration since they throw more light on the probable methods of the *agrimensores*. First, however, we shall briefly review the essential features of centuriation, as derived from the *Corpus Agrimensorum Romanorum,* by Dilke (1971) and Campbell (1996).

Land was divided into rectangular plots, or *centuriae*, by a matrix of boundaries, or *limites*, crossing at right angles. The starting point of the survey was the *tetrans* from which two main axes were set out at right angles, the *kardo maximus* (*KM*) and the *decumanus maximus* (*DM*). The parallel *limites* were known as *kardines* and *decumani* respectively. Depending on their location, the *limites* might be roads, tracks or mere baulks. Typical *centuriae* were squares of 20 *actus* but there were many non-standard squares and rectangles. A standard *centuria* comprised 400 *actus quadrati* (*a.q.*), or 200 *iugera* (one *iugerum* = two *a.q.*) Reference numbers inscribed on wooden, or stone, posts, known as *cippi,* identified plots. The siting of the *tetrans* and the orientation of the *limites* varied from place to place, though originally the *KM* was aligned N-S. Every sixth *limes* was broader than the rest and was laid out with especial care to ensure that the grid was maintained square. It was known as a *quintarius* because it enclosed five *centuriae.*

Centuriation required a survey but went beyond it in being concerned with the subsequent marking of boundaries (*limites*) many of which have survived in the modern landscape. "One of the most surprising things arising from the examination of maps and aerial photographs for traces of centuriation," wrote Chevallier (1976), "is the way in which the *limites* have survived. One is struck by the short sections of road, which do not fit in with the present day network, and turn sharply or end suddenly for no clear reason. But these stretches of road, once projected are found to be in alignment. They may be continued by a footpath or stream or by some local boundary." There are several putative centuriation systems proposed for Britain, of which we shall cite five examples. We shall not describe in detail those already published but rather concentrate on the alignment angles of the *limites* and the sizes of the plots.

East Anglia
The Norfolk centuriation almost certainly was inclined *Atan* 1/5 (11.3°) W of N (see above, Part Two). It is not immediately obvious why this angle was chosen; the flatness of the land might have been expected to allow a NSEW arrangement of *limites*. Regression analysis on the Peddar's Way, the Roman road southwards from Holme-next-the-Sea, to Castle Acre (Table 2.3, Part 2), showed it inclined *Atan* 3/7 W of N. This is not quite *Atan* 0.4 (2/5); the difference being 1.4°. But it seems likely that the centuriation was laid out in relation to this road because 23.2 − 11.3 = 11.9, which is *Atan* 0.21, that is, the centuriation virtually bisects the angle between the Peddars Way and OS grid N. The Peddar's Way keeps pace with the pre-historic Ickenield Way running along the "Western Escarpment", marking the edge of the land over 100 feet OD from the Ouse valley to the west (Dymond 1985, 29, 45-45). Dymond's map shows the escarpment inclines about 10° W of N. Thus the logical sequence is that the Ickenield Way followed the escarpment; the Peddars' Way shadowed the Ickenield Way and the centuriation was off set from the Peddars' Way. The centuriated area appears to comprise most of the county of Norfolk and there is every reason to accept Frere's suggestion that it was set out in the immediate aftermath of the Boudiccan revolt. See Figure 5.1

In south Norfolk, studies of field boundary alignments in the area crossed by the Roman road from the south (Pye Road) show they incline 4° W of N, compared to the road's 19° E of N (Dymond 1985, 47). Although Dymond did not specify whether these angles related to true N or grid N, it is almost certain they referred to the grid, because 18.435° is *Atan* 1/3 and 4.04° is *Atan* 7/99. This figure does not seem at first sight to be significant, but it is 1/20 of √2, which was a value of considerable mystic import to the ancients (Berryman 1953, 13-15) and we shall meet it again. Williamson argued this area was centuriated prior to the road's construction because in some places, notably Yaxley, it cut through existing field boundaries (Williamson 1987, 429).

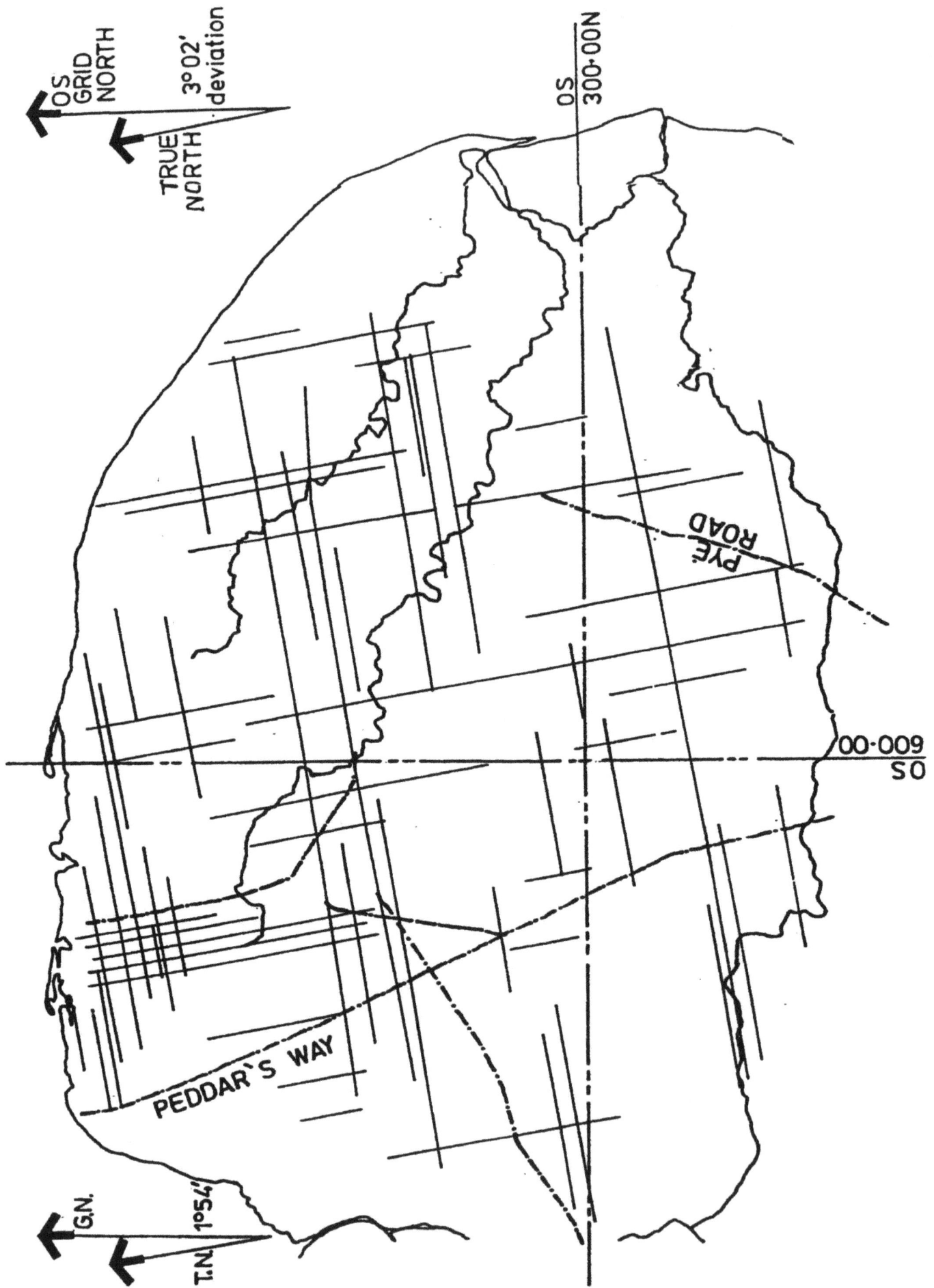

Fig. 5.1 Centurial *limites* in Norfolk
(Note the difference in the direction of true north between the east and west of the county)

Manchester

Crofton (1905) first detected evidence of centuriation at Manchester though his proposed model failed to gain general acceptance. Following the publication of Dilke's *Roman Land Surveyors* in 1971, Richardson (1983) proposed a grid more consistent with examples derived from the *Corpus Agrimensorum Romanorum*. Two key features that suggested the Manchester grid were an ancient ditch, known locally as the *Nico Ditch*, or *Mickle Ditch*, and a series of hedges along a perfectly straight line that related to the ditch as does the string to a bow. This hedgerow line was clearly a pre-enclosure feature aligned *Atan* 3/8 N of E (see part 2). It was estimated to be some 27,000 feet long and suggested the grid comprised three rows of nine squares each of 3,000 Roman feet (25 *actus*). It appeared to be confined by Hough Moss on the west, Ashton Moss on the east, the R. Medlock to the north and the Gore Brook to the south. See Figure 5.2. Richardson (1986) later showed that many 19th century field boundaries in the area tended to line up with the *limites* of this putative grid, hinting at the persistence of many intra-centurial boundaries to modern times. The geometry of the Mickle Ditch is discussed in Part 6.

A key feature of the grid was the line of a mediaeval *Saltersgate* running southwards from a ford on the R. Medlock in Bradford and now represented by Mill Street. A few yards north of this ford, the *Saltersgate* met the Manchester to Castle Shaw Roman road. According to a 13th century charter, to the southward it reached the Cornbrook (Crump 1939, 104-105) in the middle of the centuriated land. It continued through Gorton where, known as *Th' Owd Green Lane* and *The Old London Road*, it formed the township boundary and was reputedly part of a Roman route from Rochdale to Stockport (Higson, undated).

The 1848 6-inch map reveals that the distance from the hedgerow line to the Castle Shaw road, along this line is exactly 100 *actus*, or five *centuriae*. This *Saltersgate* almost certainly followed a *limes quintarius* and the length strongly suggests that the *centuriae* were not of 25 *actus*, after all but standard 20 *actus* squares. Moreover, they stand in a simple geometric relation to the local Roman roads. The evidence is as follows.

Manchester – Melandra Road.

In the past, two possible lines have been identified for this route. According to Crofton (1905, 126) the original and much corrupted line was straightened in 1733 to make Manchester - Saltersgate turnpike (Ashton Old Road) from Pin Mill Brow, Ardwick, to Seven Thorns Well, on the Droylsden – Audenshaw border. However, the Ordnance Survey have preferred the line of the 1818 Manchester – Mottram turnpike, now the A 57, Hyde Road through Denton, probably because the turnpike, unlike Ashton Old Road, points directly at Melandra and runs through Hyde township, formerly *Red Pump Street*. Moreover, a Roman coin was found close to its crossing of the R. Tame at Broomstair (Middleton 1936).

Margary (1954-57) must have been undecided about the relative merits of each for he avoided giving a line while conceding that the Manchester and Melandra forts must have been connected. Nevell (1992, 62-65) rejected the A 57 line for want of evidence of a road on that line before the 1818 turnpike, which, significantly, cut through many recent enclosures in an area that was moss land until Tudor times. He also cited old map evidence supporting Crofton's line and suggested that *Old Lane*, Openshaw, was a remnant of that Roman line. East of Droylsden, he suspected the road bent SE to join the A 57 line where it crosses the R. Tame.

Further observations support the Ashton Old Road line, but indicate that it held its direction from Ardwick and ran *directly* to Mottram Cutting (OS 398.80E 396.80N) where it met, on the same alignment, *Mottram Old Road*, the Roman road coming from Melandra, *en route* to Castle Shaw (Nevell 1992, 66). In so doing, it formed the main street of the now lost Audenshaw village and crossed the R. Tame just upstream of Shepley Bridge "at one time the only bridge across the Tame in these parts," (Middleton 1906, 341). It then followed the line of Globe Lane, Dewsnap Lane, Yew Tree Lane and Matley Lane, the latter sitting on the original alignment as it approaches Mottram Old Road. In the 18th century, these lanes, which now meet in a disjointed way, formed a through route from Shepley Bridge to Longdendale, as can be seen on Burdett's (1777) map.

In the light of this altered perspective, the 1848 6" map marked with the putative centurial grid was re-examined. It revealed that Ashton Old Road left the grid at its SE corner and between there and Ardwick it cut close to every second intersection of *limes*. When the line was redrawn to do that, it ran just a few yards to the north, along the line given by Nevell, and actually impinged on Old Lane, Openshaw. It thus ran at *Atan* 1/2 (26.5°) to the *limites*.

Manchester – Castle Shaw Road

This observation raised the question of the Manchester - Castle Shaw road's relationship to the grid. From its junction with the putative *quintarius* just north of the ford at Bradford, whose name proclaims a broad and probably substantial ford, the Castle Shaw road may be traced towards the Manchester fort along Bradford Road, Mill Street (Ancoats) and Store Street, and then projected (for its course is not clear) across Hulme from NW to SE, as Crofton (1905, 132) maintained.

Reviewing this new evidence has revealed that a standard 20 *actus* grid fits the observed features just as well as a 25 *actus* grid. The length of the probable *quintarius* (100 *actus*) would account for five standard *centuriae*, so if the grid is re-modelled and extended north of the Medlock, the system comprises two blocks of standard *centuriae*, one on either side of the *quintarius*. Each contains 25 *centuriae*, equal to one *saltus*. When this grid is drawn on to the 1848 map, a *limes* is found to coincide with Wilmslow Road, where the extant Mickle Ditch ends. See Figure 5.3

41

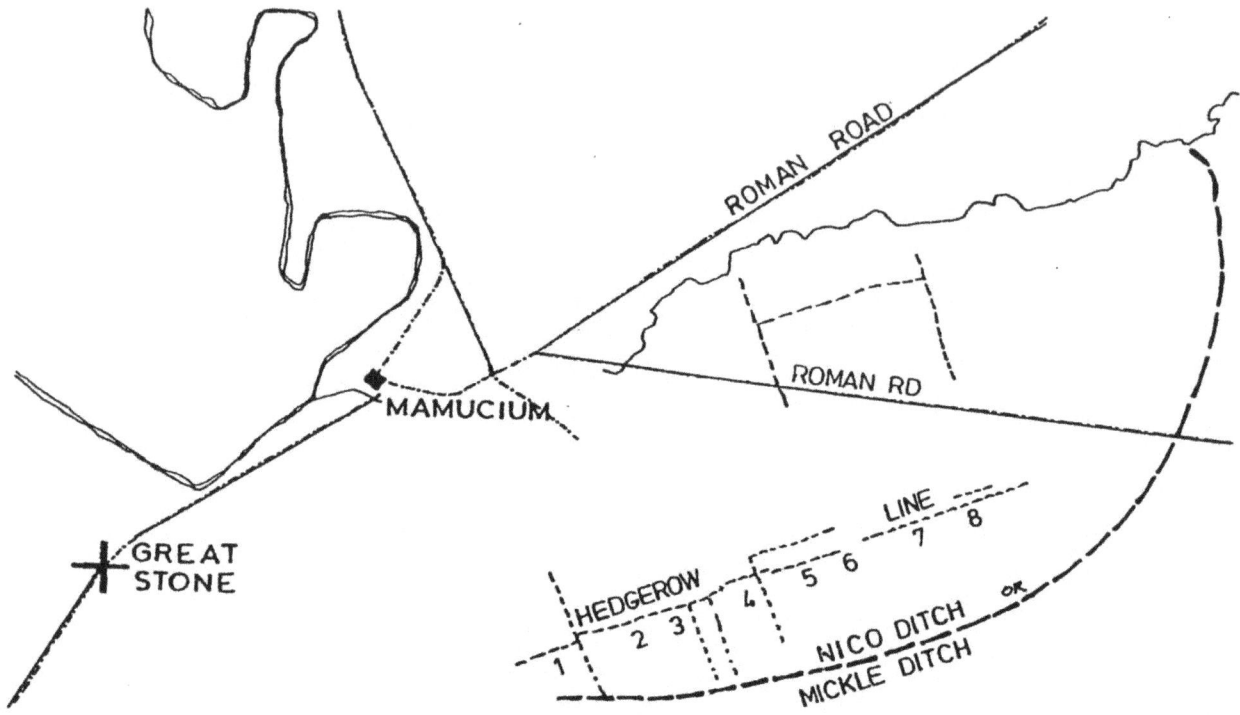

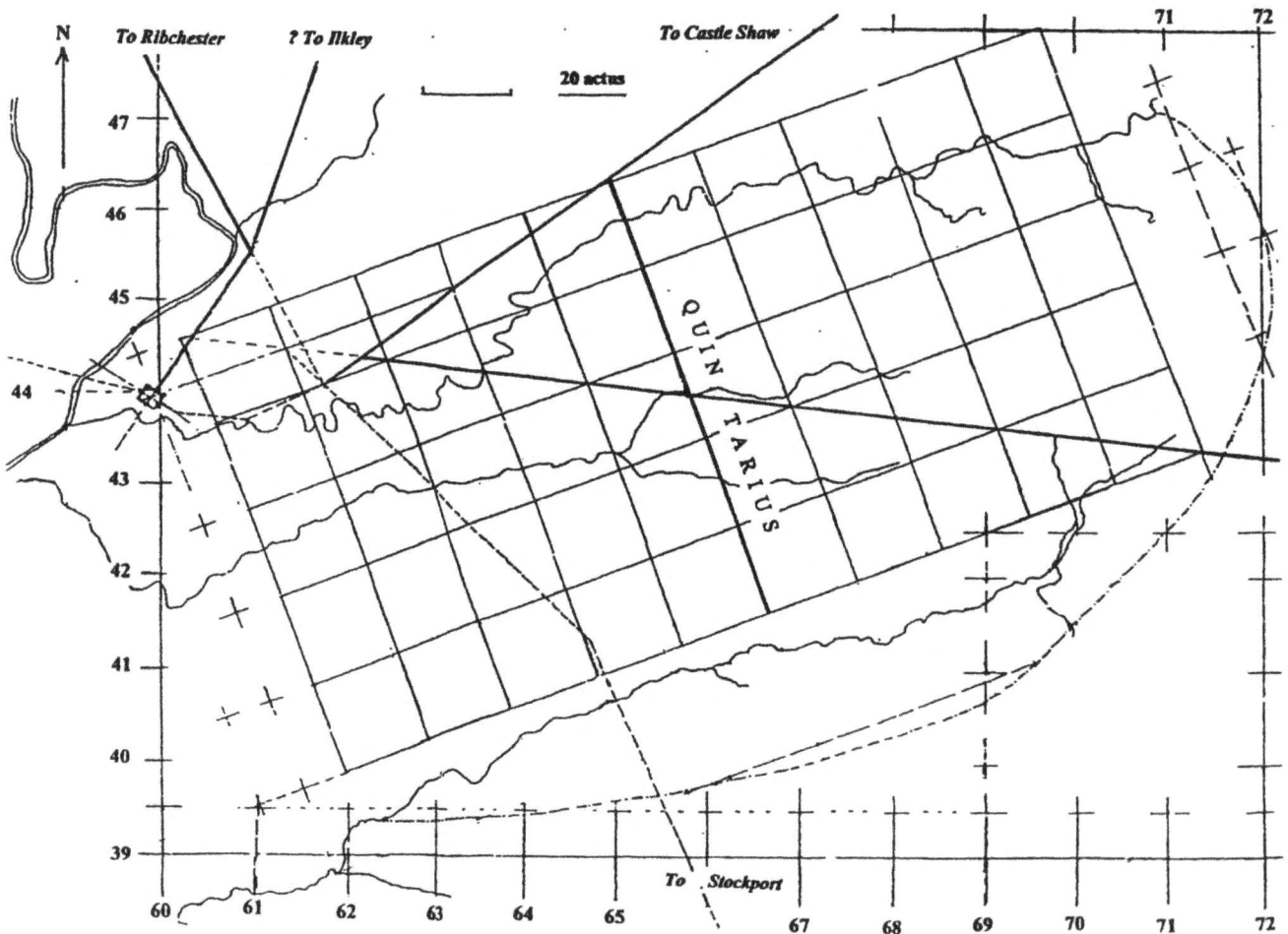

Fig. 5.2 Manchester: centuriation
(Above; the hedgerow line in relation to Roman roads and the Mickle Ditch)
(Below; the putative grid in relation to a grid based on the Chester fortress)

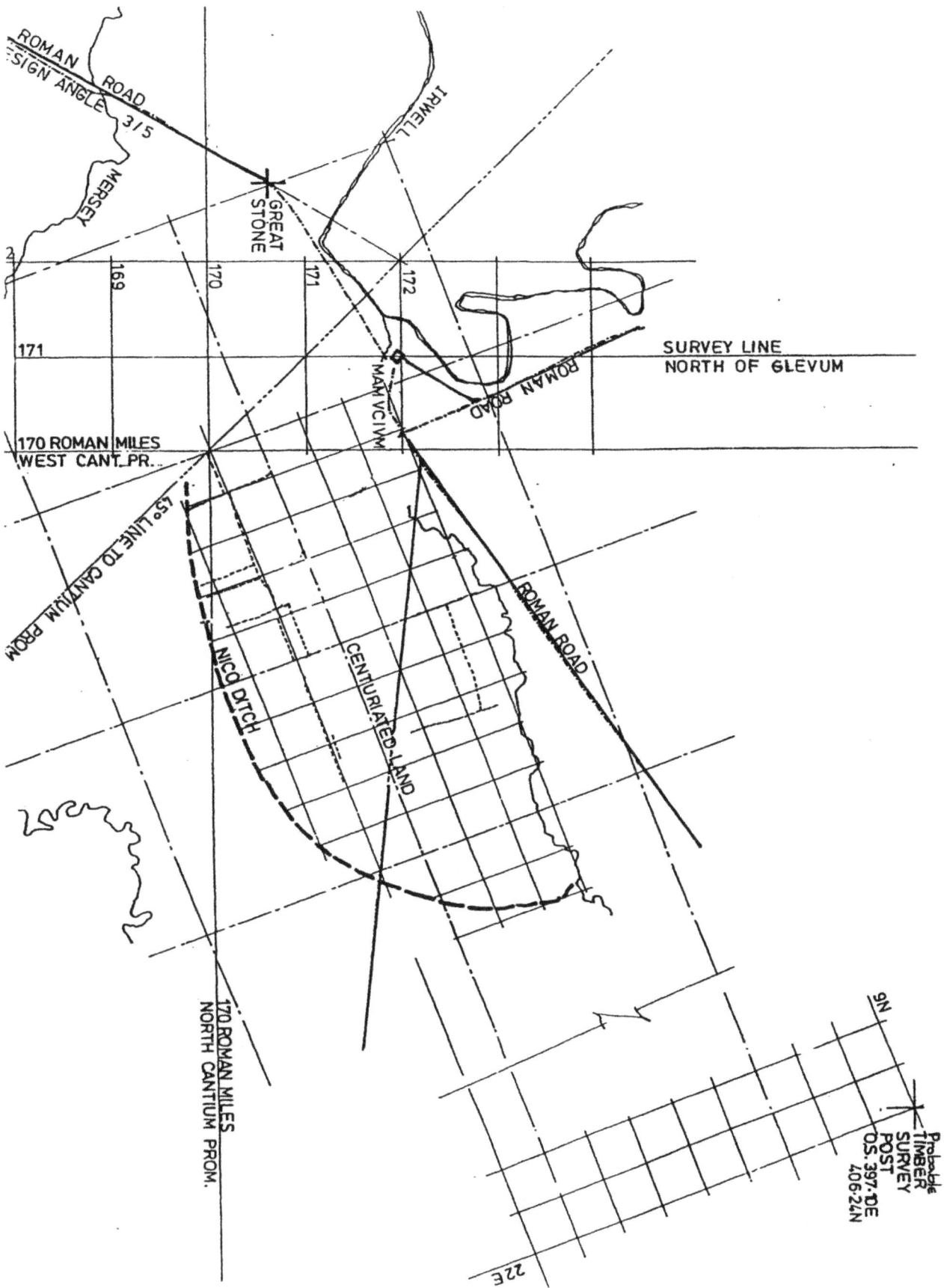

Fig 5.3 Manchester: centuriation and roads in relation to *Cantium Prom*

The angular relationship of the roads to this 20 *actus* grid is the same as to the putative 25 *actus* grid. For the Melandra road this is *Atan* ½ (see above). For the Castle Shaw Road, it is *Atan* 1/3.75, or 2/7 (15.9°), as can be seen from Figure 5.3 which shows that west of the Medlock ford the road forms the hypotenuse of a triangle whose other sides are one *centuria* and 3.75 *centuriae*. The Melandra road, as projected, meets this road in Store Street, just north of Piccadilly Station and the meeting angle is the sum of the two angles (26.5 + 15.9) or 42.4°, or *Atan* 0.913, or 913/1000. Now this is certainly not a simple ratio of integers and it is inconceivable that two roads whose alignments were presumably dictated by destination and ground conditions met at an angle which, by chance, was neatly divisible into two angles whose *Tangents* were simple integer ratios, just to make life easy for later *agrimensores*. This must mean that the centuriation and the roads were laid out at the same time. An alternative explanation is that the roads actually met an angle of *Atan* 0.9 (9/10), the 0.13 discrepancy being observer error, and the centuriation was laid out at *Atan* 1/2 to the Melandra road.

These roads connect sites of Flavian foundation and fortuitously we have supporting evidence that they date from that period. A piece of worked wood found beneath the *agger* of the Manchester-Castle Shaw road, near Oldham, was carbon-14 dated to *circa* AD 85 at the latest (Anon 1995) so the pre construction survey of this road cannot be later. This piece of wood could have been part of a surveyor's peg. The archaeologist's report indicates that it was much degraded but its shape (*circa* 10 x 2 cm) was not inconsistent with such a possibility. Its find spot was OS 397.10E 406.24N, which works out at 79.93 (80) *centuriae* E and 57.96 (58) *centuriae* north of the Chester datum. The coincidence may seem too great but should not be dismissed out of hand.

Subsequent work, reported in Part 6, has suggested that the centuriation probably extended beyond the Mickle Ditch. Moreover it is highly likely that the ancient *Great Stone* standing beside the Roman road at Stretford, (*circa* OS 380.25E 395.79N was a survey marker for both the Chester – Manchester Roman road and the centuriation. In the mid 18th century, it was moved about 50 or 60 yards "nearer Manchester" (Crofton 1905, 135-136). Crofton recorded its Roman provenance, albeit from a local myth of a giant, named Tarquin, who reputedly hurled it from the Manchester fort (a distance of 11,000 feet). See Figure 5.3.

Cumberland
We have referred in Part Two to the strong evidence of centurial *limites* in Cumberland, in the former Inglewood Forest north of Penrith and at Hayton, east of Carlisle. It was the similarity of the alignment angle of the Inglewood system, (30.96°, *Atan* 3/5, to OS grid N) to those of the Foss Way and Stane Street that suggested the existence of the same countrywide grid. Our conclusions therefore depend, in part, on the credibility of the evidence of centuriation in Cumberland. This has not been sufficient for the sceptics, notably Higham (1986) who dismissed the idea on the grounds of land quality in the Inglewood, and Caruanna (pers. comm.) who questioned the significance of the lane alignments that appear to be remnants of the grid. These arguments therefore require attention.

Higham's objection regarding land quality seemed to presume that centuriation implied intensive cereal production. In fact, it was not unknown for poor land to be centuriated, allocated to veterans and thereby provoke protest (Campbell 1996, 96). The land in Hutton, Hesket and Calthwaite is mainly a clayey loam, classed as Grade 3 by the Ministry of Agriculture, and with some drainage, it is adequate for grass, cereals and forage (Humphries 1993). It was certainly not the best land, but there was little better available and together with timber, it would have produced such crops in ancient days, albeit at lower yields. A great quantity of these products were needed by a local army with thousands of men, war-horses and draught animals, and the *Corpus Agrimensorum* notes that settlers also needed pasture and woodland (Campbell 1996, 80). There is therefore nothing "inherently" unlikely about the land immediately behind a heavily garrisoned frontier being centuriated and fully exploited for a range of produce.

The second objection is best dealt with by simply referring to the linear regression exercise on the several lanes along line AB (see above) proving that they are aligned *Atan* 3/5 W of grid N. It is inconceivable that six separate lengths of lanes overlying 45% of 14.7 km along line AB could be anything other than the remnant of a pre-enclosure feature; the angle makes it virtually certain that the line was a *limes*. The second objection also held that the quasi-geometrical arrangement of the several lanes, running parallel and at right angles, and disposed in multiples of 20 *actus*, resulted from modern enclosures. This begs the question as to why the enclosers arranged it that way. There are two significant points in this regard; the enclosure occurred over several centuries and the alignments of certain widely separated lanes are *exactly*, not roughly, coincident. See Figure 2.8.

After the Norman Conquest, the Forest was divided into a number of holdings known as serjeanties, implying the existence, or creation, of boundaries of some sort (Summerson 1991, 60). As early as the 13th century, Lord Dacre enclosed land near Middlesceugh at the northern end of line CD and the western end of line EF (Higham 1986, 94). The enclosure process almost certainly continued through the following centuries and there are references in Hesket to *Streethead* and *Lae*, i.e. *Low, Street* in 1597 and *lytle Street* in 1722 (Armstrong *et al*, undated, 206). These *streets* were either made for the enclosures or they already existed. A significant field name at Skelton in 1604 is *Mydle Sceuth yate* (Armstrong *et al*, undated, 206) which can only refer to the Skelton-Middlesceugh road on line CD, connecting Lord Dacre's 13th century enclosure to that made at Skelton 500 years later. By the mid 18th century most of Hesket, Hutton and Calthwaite was enclosed, as is revealed by a map of (Hodgkinson and Donald, circa 1770-1774) which shows the Skelton-Middlesceugh road (line CD) and its partner 40 *actus* to the east. Also marked are *Itonfield Street, Low Street, Plumpton Street* and other tracks across the unenclosed parts of Calthwaite and Hesket.

44

Further observations

The track shown on the Hogkinson and Donald map running from Hutton Row to Thomas Close, at the southern end of *Itonfield Street* has now largely gone, but four clues indicate that it marked a major *limes* along line AB.

i. A crop mark in a pasture at OS NY 4445 4010, consisting of a wide, dry, strip, margined by rushes, was photographed by the author in 1980 before the field was severely disturbed and the feature lost. It appears to be the base of an *agger*. See plates 1 and 2. This crop mark is over 20 feet wide, enough for it to qualify as a *cardo maximus* under an Augustan law (Chevallier 1976, 66).

ii. The course of the *Lyne* Beck, which runs along line AB between Morton Mill Road and *Streethead*, is straddled by many large stones, not otherwise abundant in the locality, suggestive of disturbed kerbs and metalling.

iii. The name of the Lyne Beck, forming the parish boundary, may be derived from *limes*, as in Cheshire, where it is often associated with boundary roads (Dogdson 1970, 4).

iv. At Low Grange, near *Streethead*, two fields at OS NY 4301 4200, abutting on to line AB, were named *Far Street Close* and *Near Street Close* in 1817, (1817 Estate map of Itonfield, County Record Office, Carlisle).

In summary, the several lanes along the lines AB, CD, and EF were laid down over a period of 50 to 500 years, almost certainly because they were set upon pre-existing features. That ancient lanes existed and were incorporated into the 1819 enclosure is clear from the Award, which lists the proposed new roads. Laithes Road, for example, "Beginning at the *ancient gate* in Catterlen Hall Estate and leading northwards and westwards to the east end of an *ancient road* which leads to Laithes Bridge (Anon 1819). This "ancient" road, from Skelton to Newton Reigny, is the continuation of *Mydle Sceuth Yate*.

The area immediately south of Carlisle is now crossed by roads, which, in a general way, fan out, from the town towards the *limites* of the Inglewood system; that is to Durdar, to Brisco, to Cumwhinton and to Cotehill and the two main Roman roads, to Old Carlisle and Penrith. But there are some minor lanes aligned with the Inglewood grid and Chancellor Ferguson, a 19th century authority with an immense knowledge of the antiquities of the Carlisle area outlined the course of a "pre-Roman" road west of the city from Etterby Wath, on the Eden, "up Willow Holme", by existing lanes, to Upperby and thence to Wreay and so to Penrith (Ferguson 1886). This line would follow the *limes* five *centuriae* west of line AB which, on the evidence of the width of the crop mark at Morton Mill (see above), was at least a *limes quintarius*. Ferguson's road would be, therefore, also a *limes quintarius* whose more robust construction enabled it to survive sufficiently well to be detectable to Ferguson.

The Inglewood grid was probably confined to south of Newbiggin Road, between the Caldew and the R. Eden. The area east of the Carlisle-Brougham road was almost certainly centuriated because three long boundary hedges, extant at the end of the 17th century, appear to have marked certain *limites*. They are shown on Bowey's map of 1715 (Bowey 1715). Although this map is free-hand drawn, the length and general direction of these hedges can be determined from their relationship to features identifiable on the modern map. One "old hedge" accompanied the *High Street* between Cotehill and Aiketgate, previously cited by Richardson (1986) running parallel to, and probably co-incident with, the Inglewood *limes* 10 *centuriae* east of line AB. The spacing indicates it was a *quintarius*. Another, the "Castle Hewen Boundary Hedge", also parallel to AB, ran about one *centuria* nearer that *limes* for over a mile from the centre of Tarn Wadling to the slate quarry north of Barrock Fell. The modern map shows that this hedge ran nine *centuriae* parallel and east of line AB. Connecting both at right angles was another "Old Hedge" from the slate quarry going ENE roughly 15 *centuriae* south of Stanwix to just north of the *Tackengate Stone*. Moreover, there was yet another long hedge, the "Barrock Fold Hedge", running along the seventh *limes* east of AB from Scalesceugh to *Court Thorn*, on the Roman Road north of High Hesket village. Court Thorn was an ancient meeting point where the feudal lords and tenants of the Inglewood Forest met to transact Forest business (Hutchinson, 1794-97, 504) and it proves to be 20 *actus* north of line EF. It is very likely that a centurial stone once stood here. The boundary of the Carlisle Dean and Chapter land seems to have roughly followed another *limes* from Wragmire towards the R. Eden. See Figure 5.4. A folk memory of another "ancient British" track between Tarn Wadling and Aiketgate was recorded by a local inhabitant in recent times (McGillivray, undated).

The main area of the Inglewood centuriation lies along the River Petteril, the origin of whose name has puzzled scholars. Breeze (2001) has now concluded that it refers to a "rectangle, square; rectangular or square ...", being derived from Old British, *petryal*, square, for which there are examples in Wales. Breeze discusses this interpretation in terms of Roman forts or ancient graves, but the most likely explanation is that the river flowed through land that was clearly marked out in *centuriae*. Some remains were almost certainly detectable on the ground at the enclosure of 1818, for a new farmstead in Hutton, the property of the Duke of Devonshire, was named Devonshire Square. It stands plumb in the centre of a putative *centuria* (Richardson 1982, 68).

East and west of Carlisle

Studies in Mediterranean countries have revealed separate, superimposed centuriation systems running at divergent angles in some places (Bradford 1957, 136). Previously, Richardson (1986, 76) speculated that at Hayton, east of Carlisle, two parallel E-W roads, 20 *actus* apart and one named *How Street*, were vestiges of a separate system. The following observations suggest that this system, aligned on the cardinal points of the OS grid, may have been associated with the modern Warwick Road which approaches Carlisle from due east, probably on a Roman line (see Part 8). How Street lies along the 557.00 northing, 10 *actus* (1/2 *centuria*) south of Wall Knowe.

45

Plates

**Plate 1: Crop mark of putative limes showing as a light strip behind the pylon in the centre.
Morton Mill Road, Calthwaite, OS 344.45E 540.10N**

Plate 2: The same feature at ground level

BARROCK FOLD BOUNDARY HEDGE

BOUNDARY HEDGE

HIGH STREET

OLD HEDGE

HIGH STAND PLANTATION

BARROCK FELL

CASTLE HEWEN BOUNDARY HEDGE

RIVER PETTERIL

TARN

WADLING

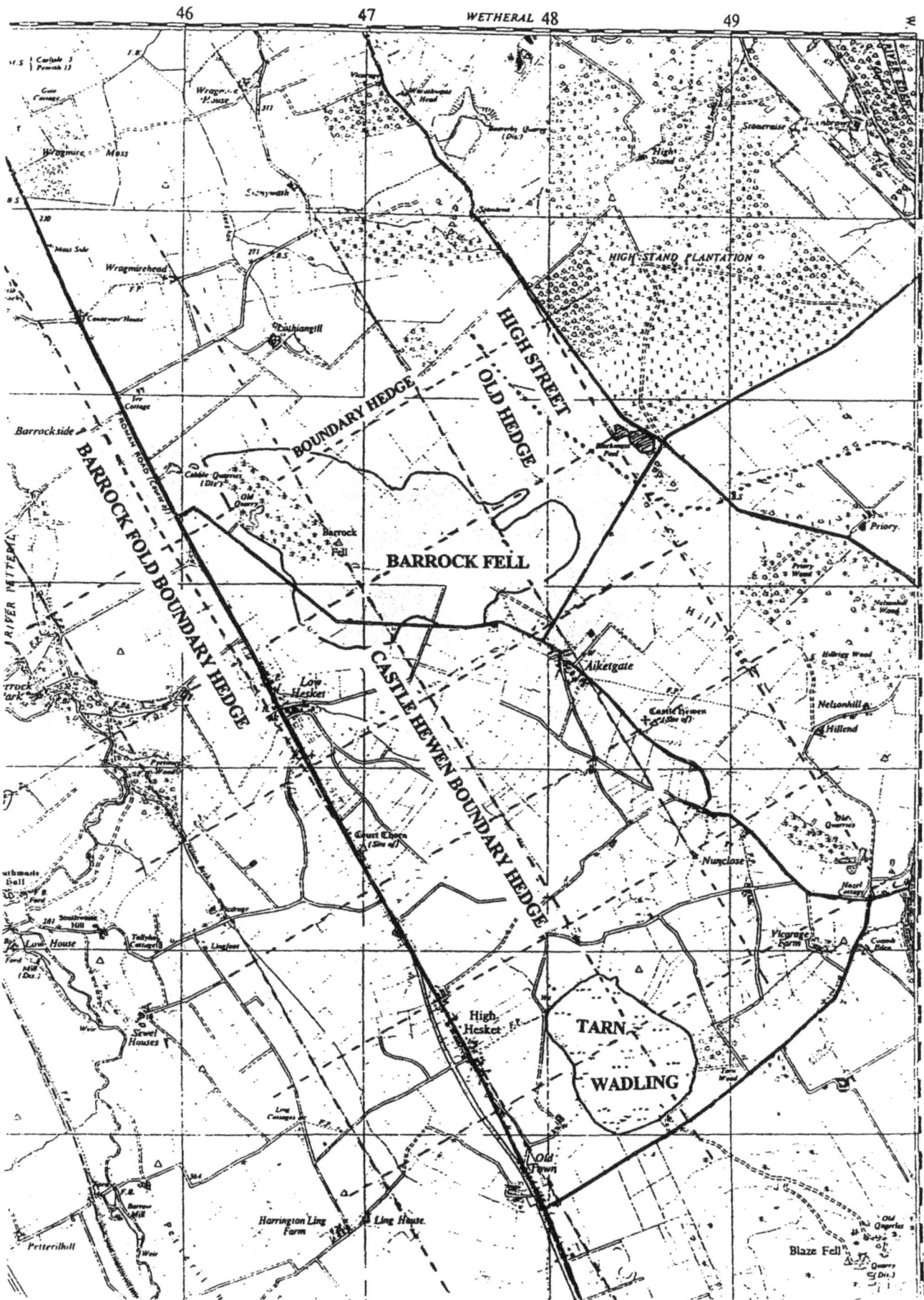

Fig 5.4 Cumberland: *limites* **in existence in Hesket** *circa* **1700 – after Bowie**

1. Newbiggin Road is 139.4, (say 140 *actus* or seven *centuriae*) south of, and parallel to, Warwick Road as it approaches the Roman city. It runs along the 5100 northing for 2.3 km. from Durdar, to Newbiggin Hall (OS 343.00E 551.00N).
2. A straight line southwards from Carlisle (easting 4099) follows the road through Blackwell to Newbiggin Road at Durdar.

Apart from the alignments of Warwick Road, Blackwell Road and Newbiggin Road, there is no other hint of an NSEW centuriation in the road and field layout west of the Eden and north of Newbiggin Road. West of Carlisle, however, a vast number of field boundaries and roads in the rectangle defined by Moorhouse, Great Orton, Thursby, Parton, Aikton and Little Bampton are aligned on the cardinal points. This may be due to land relief, particularly the drumlins and westward flowing streams, but it is curious that the A 596 road through Low Whinow, west of Thursby, aligns exactly with Newbiggin Road along the NY 5100 northing. Moreover, the N-S roads of several villages in this area occur at significant multiples of *actus* west of the Stanwix-Durdar easting; *viz*. Aikton (355, or 17.75 *centuriae*), Oughterby (300, or 15 *centuriae*) and Great Orton (200, or 10 *centuriae*). See Figure 5.5.

Old Penrith
We have dealt with the alignments of the Carlisle – Low Borrowbridge road in Part Two and shown that between Reagill and Stanwix the alignment bears Atan ½ W of grid N, with secondary alignments taking the causeway westwards to pass the fort of Old Penrith. Passing a little southwards of High Hesket, at OS 348.10 543.38, this alignment change begins by a slight westward shift to Thiefside Hill (OS 348.65 541.50) from whence the next section goes straight to Old Penrith. The field boundaries from Thiefside all the way to Plumpton are clearly based upon this road line, though it is possible that these are modern enclosures. Incidentally, the Roman causeway here lay about 20 metres west of the modern road and until the 1970s was visible at Aikbank Common (OS 348.70 541.25). The agger is still visible where it climbs a steep bank north of Bulls Head Farm (OS 348.95 540.00).

From the disposition of the fields and lanes south of the Old Penrith fort, four observations can be made. See Figure 5.6.

1. Plumpton crossroads are two *centuriae* south of the fort's *via principalis*.
2. Low Street, suspected by Ferguson (1890, 44) to be the pre-Roman track from Etterby to Penrith, runs two *centuriae* west of the Roman road.
3. The alignment of the EW arm of the Plumpton crossroads may be projected some 7 km. eastwards to the R. Eden where the last 2 km, from Scatterbeck to the river, forms the perfectly straight Lazonby-Great Salkeld parish boundary.
4. At right angles to this line and slightly over six *centuriae* to the east of, and parallel to, the main Roman road by the fort, runs a modern road (OS 354.05 538.00 to OS 353.37 540.59). This is near the line of the mediaeval *via regia* of two Holm Cultram charters (*circa* 1200) discussed by Wilson (1976). This road went to Armathwaite and separated Lazonby demesne from Brownrigg, within the manor of Lazonby. Wilson surmised that the via regia lay east of this modern road, but careful reading of his quotes from the charters reveals that this was only because he guessed that a certain arable plot must have been in the townfields of Lazonby. See Figure 5.5.

This is strong *prima facie* evidence of another centuriation system near the Old Penrith fort; aligned on the road and encompassing a tract of land between the rivers Petteril and Eden. Its northerly limit, east of the Petteril, would appear to be at the southern terminus of the Inglewood system but that to the south is not clear. It is related to the Inglewood system by a limes, three centuriae east of line AB, now marked by a modern road running into Low Street, just NE of the fort, but does not appear to have extended further west than this road.

The significance of centuriation in Cumberland. A major problem facing Roman road research, whether or not associated with centuriation, is the absence of any agreed criteria for judging thevalidity of evidence. Straight modern road alignments with angled shifts; *street* place-names, coincident parish boundaries and mediaeval references to saltways and *magnae viae* are generally accepted as significant clues. But none, taken singly, are conclusive and the sceptic may dismiss any combination of them, along with the remnants of *aggers*, kerbs and ditches, should their discovery prove inconvenient.

Centuriation in the immediate hinterland of the Wall should not be surprising. Manning has argued convincingly that transport costs obliged Roman forces to obtain as much sustenance as possible locally (Manning 1975). He quoted a study by Petrokovits (1960) to the effect that a legion needed a territorium of 8,645 acres. This is possibly quite an under-estimate for it gives a "stocking rate", to use a farming term, of about 1.4 men per acre without considering the needs of draught and cavalry animals and non-combatants. In the same paper, Manning estimated that 700 acres were needed simply for the corn for 480 men. According to the evidence cited by Breeze and Dobson (1976, 140, 155), in Hadrian's time, the Wall forts from Birdoswald to Bowness housed units with a nominal strength of 3,808 infantry and 1,408 cavalry. Assuming that half as many remounts (reserve animals) were needed, the western Wall would account for some 2,000 horses. Maintained on rough pasture close to the forts in summer at one per two acres, they would need 4,000 acres. When not at grass, in the winter or when on standby for action or in training, they would need about 5 kgs. hay and 4 kgs. grain per head daily. For 250 days feed per year, these horses would need about 2,600 metric tons of each, and assuming a hay yield of one metric ton per acre, a similar number of acres were needed. Piggot (1992) has estimated that a chariot horse needed the annual barley produce of five acres;

48

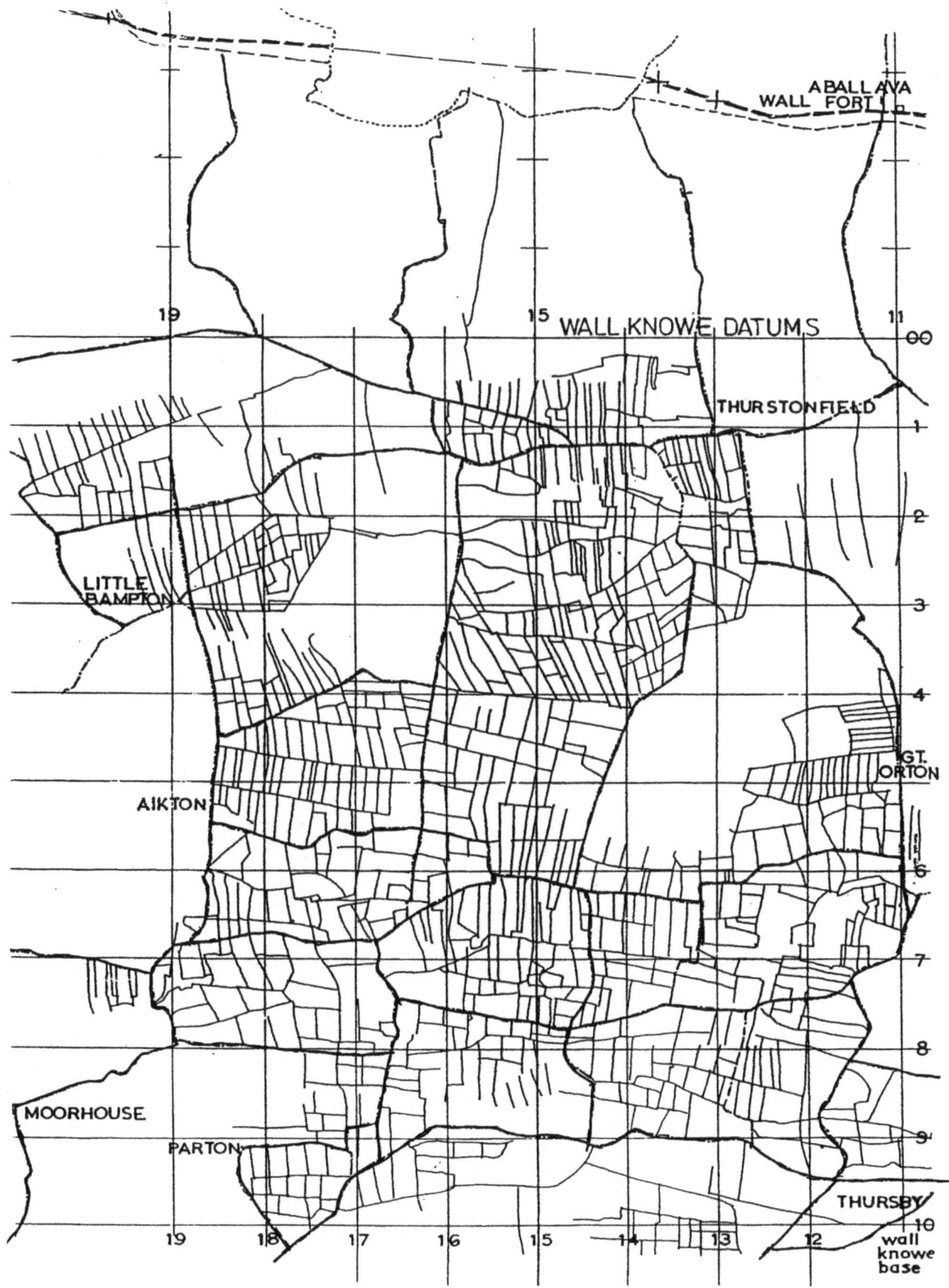

Fig 5.5
Field boundaries west of Carlisle in relation to a NSEW centurial grid based on Wall Knowe

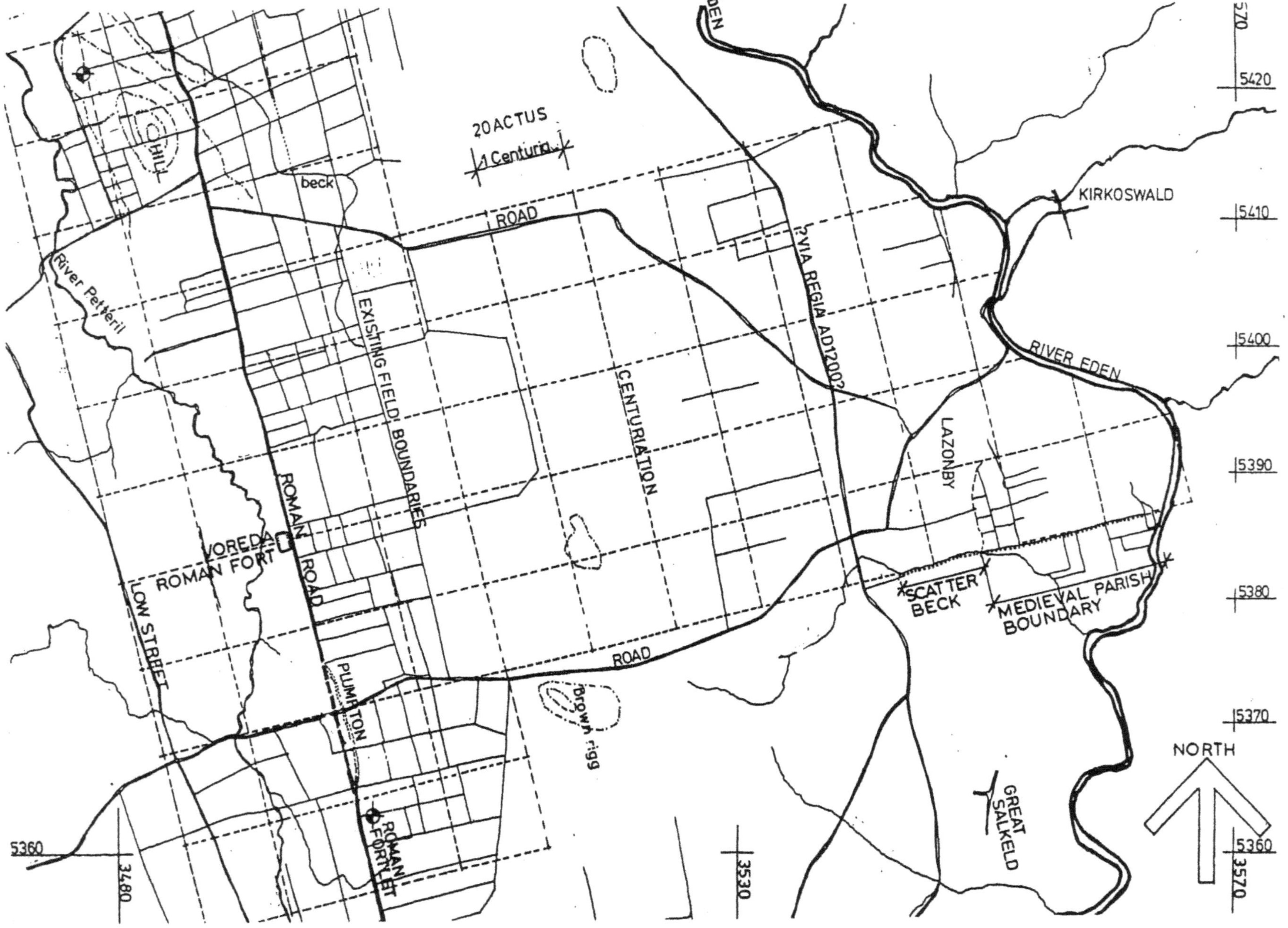

Fig 5.6 Probable centurial *limites* at Old Penrith, Cumberland
(Note how many field boundaries align with the putative grid)

50

so another 10,000 acres should be added. A round figure of 17,000 acres might not be far off the mark. To this must be added the corn requirement of the men, which on Manning's figures, needed some further 5,553 acres, giving a total of 22,153 acres. This does not take into account the needs of draught, breeding and growing animals, non-combatants and civilians, nor of the central wall and coastal forts, nor of those at Old Penrith, Old Carlisle, Brougham and Kirkby Thore. It is probably no exaggeration to say that the Cumberland Wall forts alone needed food for man and beast from at least 35,000 acres. This is equivalent to the combined 19th century arable and pasture acreages of Dalston (10,500), Hesket (15,000) and Skelton (11,000) (Humphries 1993, 640).

This demand, superimposed on the natives' needs, and the formidable transport costs in meeting it from outside the area, explains why the Roman authorities could not afford to be choosy about the quality of land near the Wall. It is likely that every available acre was pressed into use with customary Roman vigour.

Cirencester

The evidence from Norfolk and Cumbria points to roads having been used as base lines for subsequent centuriation whereas at Manchester the centuriation appears to have been set out at the same time as the road network. The disposition of certain modern field boundaries at Cirencester suggested that, in that area, the roads had also formed the skeleton upon which centuriation systems were based. *See* Figure 5.6. The salient features of this area are as follows.

i.   The Foss Way approaches Cirencester from the south-west but instead of holding to its mean survey line, it swings eastwards to enter the town. The alignment node where this swing starts is exactly ten *centuriae* from the road linking Tetbury to the Foss Way.

ii. The last Foss Way alignment before the town continues beyond it as the first section of Akeman Street, from which the Foss Way's northwards continuation branches just east of the town.

iii. Twenty *centuriae* south of Akeman Street, and parallel to it, runs the Highworth -Farringdon road, with many of the field boundaries in between conforming to a standard centurial grid.

iv. Ermine Street departs north westerly from the town at *Atan* 3/5 W of N. This section lies on the "planning grid" (*Atan* 3/5 W of N) 240 *centuriae* from *Cantium Prom*, while the town itself stands at the intersection of the two "planning grid" lines, one 240 *centuriae* from *Cantium Prom* and the other 40 *centuriae*.

Hampshire and the Isle of Wight

The NW coast of the Isle of Wight is aligned *Atan* 3/5 N of E and a line drawn at that angle through Gurnard may be projected to the Roman fort at Portchester (OS 462.42E 104.72N). Gurnard is the site of a Roman signal tower standing opposite the terminus of a Roman road on the mainland. The distance from Portchester to Gurnard along the line is 510, or 15 x 34, *actus*, and when the line is projected for another 510 *actus*, it reaches Totland (OS 431.35 086.07N). The line appears to have formed a survey datum for the rest of the island because certain villas are placed parallel, or perpendicularly to it, at multiples of 34 *actus*. Our measurements were made from the OS 1:25,000 and six inch maps upon which the grid (*Atan* 3/5 N of E) was drawn using a parallel motion drawing board.

In terms of the angled grid they are sited as follows.

i.   From the line of Bowcombe, to that of Newport is 34 x 3 (102) *actus* east, and to the Brading line is 34 x 9 (306) *actus*.

ii. From the line of Newport to that of Brading is therefore 34 x 6 (204) *actus*.

iii. From the line of Gurnard to that of Clatterford is 34 x 6 (204) *actus* southwards.

iv. From the line of Gurnard to that of Brading is 34 x 12 (408) *actus* southwards.

From these data a grid of squares can be drawn can be drawn. Figure 5.7 a shows such a grid with the lines at 102 (34 x 3) *actus* intervals.

When a similar grid is extended over Hampshire and west Sussex, but slightly adjusted to centre on Portchester, a similar picture emerges. The distances of certain villas, in *actus* from Portchester, are as follows.

i.   Northwards: Stroud at 34 x 9 (306) and Sparsholt at 34 x 27 (918).

ii. Southwards: Langstone, Chilgrove, and Warren Down, all at 34 x 3 (102) and then Fishbourne at almost 34 x 9 (306) and Sidlesham at 34 x 15 (510).

iii. Eastwards: Crookhorn, at almost 34 x 6 (204), West Meon and Leigh Park, 34 x 9 (306): Stroud and Pitland at 34 x 15 (510), Chilgrove at almost 34 x 18 (612), Bignor at 34 x 30 (1020)

It is noticeable that with the exception of Stroud and Chilgrove on the mainland, and Brading on the island, all of which lie on two "planning grid" co-ordinates, the villas stand on only one line. This probably means that while a site on two co-ordinates was desirable, being on one was preferable to not being on any

51

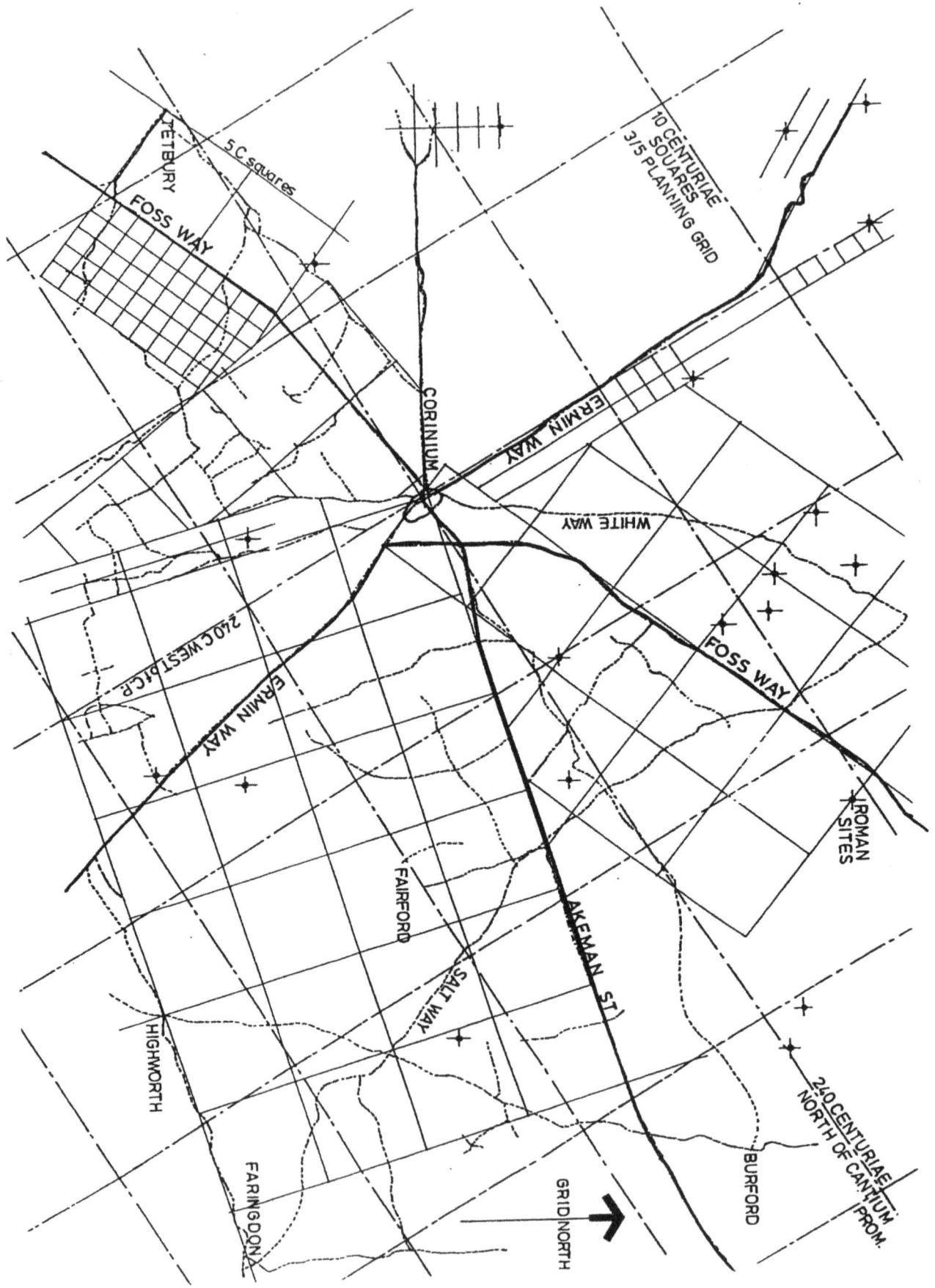

Fig 5.6   Probable centurial *limites* and Roman road alignments at Cirencester

Labels visible on figure:
TETBURY
FOSS WAY
5 C squares
10 CENTURIAE SQUARES 3/5 PLANNING GRID
CORINIUM
ERMIN WAY
WHITE WAY
FOSS WAY
240 C WEST BICP
ERMIN WAY
AKEMAN ST
SALT WAY
FAIRFORD
HIGHWORTH
FARINGDON
ROMAN SITES
240 CENTURIAE NORTH OF CANTIUM PROM.
BURFORD
GRID NORTH

It is possible to identify putative survey points within the island. Figure 5.8 shows how lines set at a right angle from Gurnard reach Castle Hill and a point near Brading just north of Centurion's Copse (no Roman connection; the name is derived from St. Urien). When a line connects the last point with Castle Hill, a 3:4:5 right angle triangle is created with a unitary dimension of 120 *actus*, i.e., sides of 320, 480 and 600 *actus*. The 480 *actus* line cuts the aligned 34 *actus* grid at regular 120 *actus* intervals. A line from Gurnard to St. Catherine's cuts the 600 *actus* line perpendicularly.

The significance of these observations lies in the light they throw on the probable practical steps in the survey. The Portchester – Gurnard – Totland line could be projected from the mainland survey by sightings across the Solent, and the rest of the 34 *actus* grid likewise. The 480 *actus* Gurnard – Centurion's Copse line marked at 120 *actus* intervals enabled the line projected from the mainland to be cross-checked and tied down, thus ensuring that the grid on the island did not suffer distortion and error by being extended from across the water.

At first sight, a 34 *actus* square does not seem at all plausible. If, however, each side were halved, it would give four plots of 17 *actus* square. This dimension does not appear any more plausible and Dilke (1972, 85) did not include it in a list of non-standard *centuriae*, though 21 x 21 *actus* squares (220.5 *iugera*) were observed at Acelum and Tarvisium. These were the only examples of a fractional area value, so a 17 x 17 square is not impossible. Indeed, it becomes very plausible when we consider how it might have been subdivided, for it would have had an area of 144.5 *iugera*, suggesting linear dimensions of 12 x 12 units, (12 x 12 = 144) and a *centuria* divided into 12 plots of 12 *iugera* seems a convenient arrangement. The unit turns out to be 170 feet, or 1.42 *actus*. The attraction of this solution is that 1.42 is √2; a number of mystical significance to the ancients as we have already remarked. So when set out as a square, the *iugerum* of two *a.q.* has a linear dimension of √2 *actus*. Moreover, there is a link to modern measures.

Roman plots of one *iugera* (170 x 170 feet) are too small to have been practical but the dimension can be divided into ten lengths of 17 Roman feet, a length that equals the rod, pole or perch, of 16.5 statute feet. The term "perch" is derived from the Latin, *pertica*, a measuring rod, and though originally thought to have been synonymous with the ten-foot *decempeda*, the same term described rods varying from 12 feet in the south of England to 22 feet in the north (Dilke 1971, 137, 210). A *pertica* of 17 Roman feet is therefore quite probable. Forty of them made 680 Roman feet, or 660 statute feet, or 220 yards, the furlong. Thus we may surmise that the Anglo-Saxons plough furrow (furlong) took exactly one third of the linear dimension of the 17 *actus* square (2040 / 680 = 3). Four rods make 66 feet or 22 yards, or one chain. An area of one chain by one furlong comprises one statute acre.

The 17 *actus* square could therefore be split into nine blocks of 16 *iugera*, each of whose sides is 4 x 170 = 680 Roman feet. This is 40 perches square, or ten acres, which divides into ten one-acre strips measuring 4 by 40 rods. The whole *centuria* comprised 90 acres. It is likely, therefore, that our modern land measurements, probably defined at nearby Winchester in the late Saxon period (Connor 1987, 39), are derived from the Roman landscape of Hampshire, where 17 *actus centuriae* were common. They were probably worked by ox teams that ploughed the length of one of these plots, and a length of four rods in the other direction was probably regarded as a day's work. It may have been customary even before the advent of the Saxons to measure the ploughed land in units of 4 by 40 perches (160 sq. perches). The Roman *pertica* lost six inches to become the statute perch and thus the 4 by 40 perch unit became the statute acre, This evolution argues for a continuity of farming practice and land management in southern England from antiquity into the mediaeval period.

****

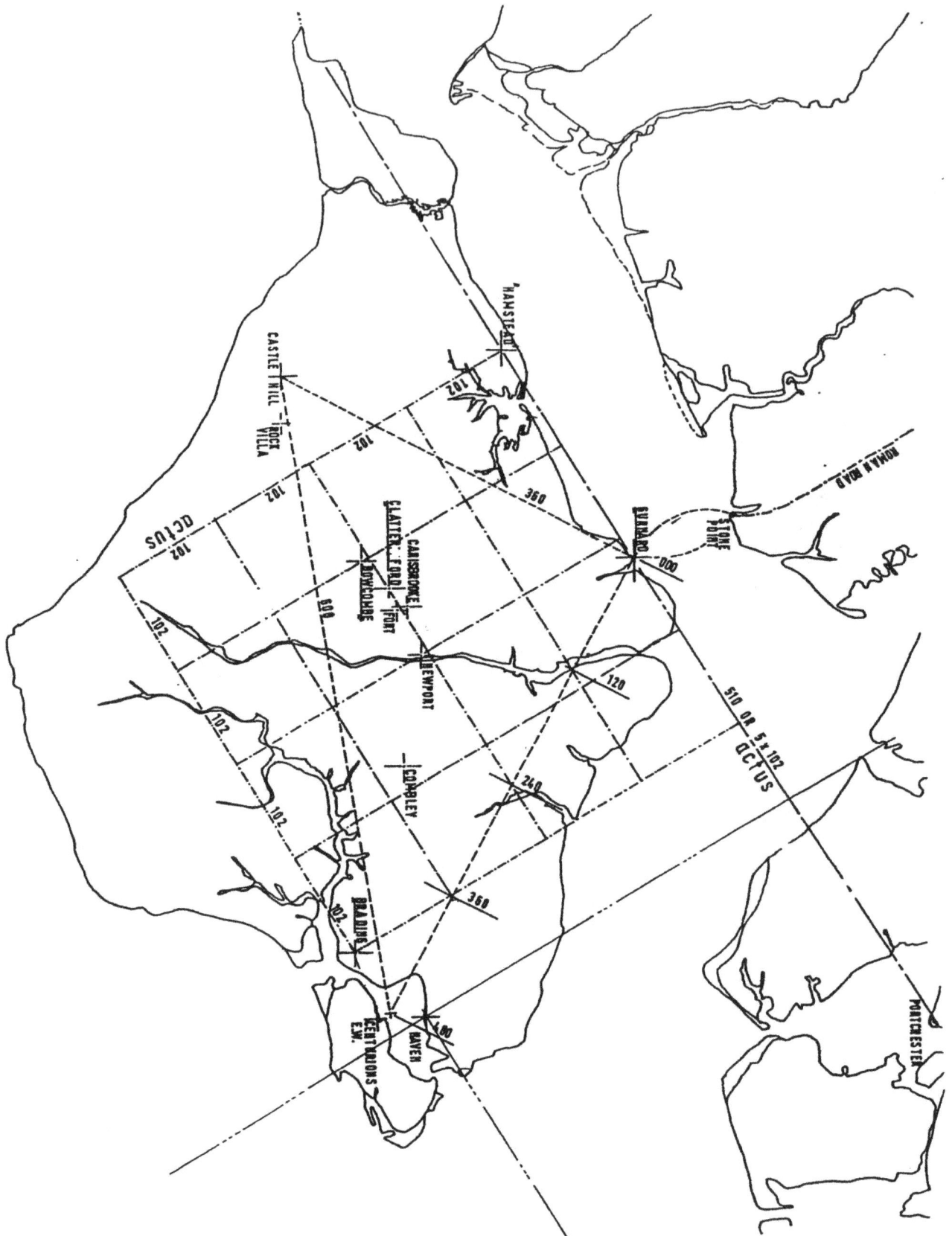

Fig 5.7 Isle of Wight: villas in relation to a probable 34 *actus* centurial grid

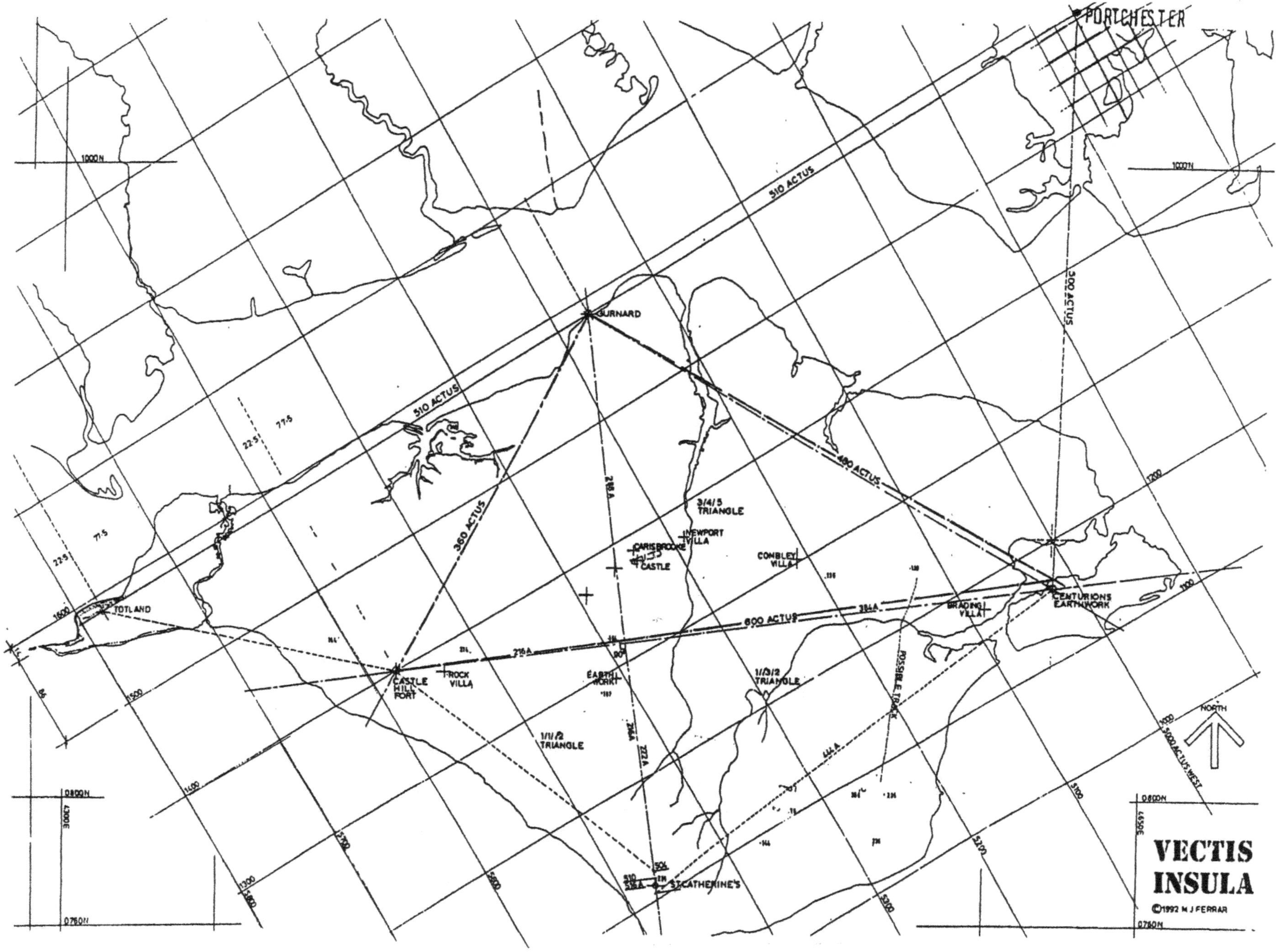

Fig 5.8 Isle of Wight: Probable basic survey triangle with dimensions.

PART SIX

EUCLIDIAN GEOMETRY IN THE LANDSCAPE:

THE MICKLE DITCH AT MANCHESTER

Having cited evidence of certain triangles being planned into the landscape and having surmised that it was an expression of Pythagorean mysticism, we now consider another ancient landscape feature that bears the indelible signature of *agrimensores* who applied Euclidian geometry for aesthetic, as well as for practical, reasons.

The Mickle, or *Nicker,* or *Nico*, Ditch, at Manchester, was a ditch and earthen earth bank following a five mile curved course across what are now the south east Manchester suburbs, from Platt Chapel on Wilmslow Road, to Ashton Moss. Though clearly depicted on the 1848 OS six-inch map, it has now been largely destroyed. See Figure 6.1. Addison Crofton (1885) recorded the tradition that it was made in AD 870 by an Anglo-Saxon army from Manchester, each man digging his own body length during one night prior to a battle with the Danes, after which the ditch was filled with the slain. He suspected the term "Nicker" was derived either from the Norse word for a water sprite, or the Anglo-Saxon, *noecan*, cognate with the Latin, *necare,* to kill, in reference to the battle. Esdaile (1892) identified it as the *magna fossa* of a deed of 1150 but pointed out that it predated the advent of the Danes because it formed the boundary of the Saxon townships of Withington and Rusholme. He noted that the ditch lay south of the bank and suspected it was a Saxon work for draining Ashton Moss.

Crofton (1905) concluded it was Roman. He cited several references to its existence in the Middle Ages; the *Mykel Diche* in Audenshaw (1200), the *Milk Wall* at Slade (1270), the *Mekel dyche* in Rusholme (1317) and the *Muchil Dich* at Reddish (1322). He dismissed the idea that it was a defence work and correctly so, since it would have been indefensible. He noted that its dimensions in various sections seemed to reflect Roman decimal measurements and in tracing the its course from west to east, drew attention to its serving as a manor boundary separating Rusholme and Gorton on the north from Levenshulme, Reddish and Denton to the south. At Debdale Clough it stopped serving as a boundary and "from that point takes a northward curve…" But at that point Crofton broke off to discuss another matter.

Melland (1936) summarised and supplemented these observations. He wrote that behind Platt Chapel the ditch was six feet deep and that at Melland Fields, Gorton, the bank top was five feet above the ditch bottom. He then made an error that has been much repeated. From Debdale Clough he thought the ditch followed the course of a tributary stream coming from Ashton Moss through Droylsden in whose rectory garden he thought the ditch could be detected. In doing this, he transferred the line of the ditch from its course along what is now seen to be obviously an arc of a circle, to the common boundary of Clayton and Ashton under Lyne that was established in the early 15th century (Bowman 1960, 43-46). Melland did, however, concede its possible Roman origin, citing the distinguished scholar, O.G.S. Crawford who dated it to the end of the Roman period. In *A History of Droylsden* Speake and Witty (1953) repeated Melland's view.

Richardson (1983), in proposing a revised system of centuriation at Manchester, drew attention to the fact that, on the 1848 map, the ditch's curving line in Debdale Clough can be projected by eye across the southern end of Lumb Lane, Audenshaw, to another curved portion of extant ditch by the Snipe Inn, Audenshaw (SJ 9180 9807). (The recent motorway works beside the Snipe Inn revealed this ditch to be over ten feet deep and bottomed with large stones. It is now destroyed). Then after a short break, on the same arc, there is another section across the end of Benny Lane, Droylsden, (SJ 9175 9915) and then after another break, the now largely filled-in but quite detectable, ditch along the western side of the track from Cinderland Hall, Littlemoss, (SJ9135 9975) to the top of the dingle draining into the R. Medlock.

Nevell (1992) reviewed the subject and rejected both Melland's and Richardson's line north of Debdale Clough, preferring instead an intermediary access to Ashton Moss along Lumb Lane, Audenshaw. More recently, Richardson has restated his view that the ditch was a Roman boundary (Richardson 2001a), but see below.

We shall now set out evidence that the Mickle Ditch was laid out in Roman dimensions by surveyors who applied Greek theorems familiar to the Romans but almost certainly not to their successors in Britain before the Renaissance. We shall also suggest that the ditch was not a boundary but a land drain.

Methods
We used the relevant sections of the 1848 OS six-inch map and the modern 1:25,000 map, which were placed on a surveyor's parallel motion drawing board and overlaid with tracing paper. The adjacent portions of the 1848 map have undergone some shrinkage such that it is no longer possible to align them side-by-side, so the relevant features were redrawn by a professional draughtsman (MJF) on a single large sheet that incorporated the corrections made with the aid of the 1:25000 map. The geometric features of the ditch line were then abstracted from the new plan and measured accordingly.

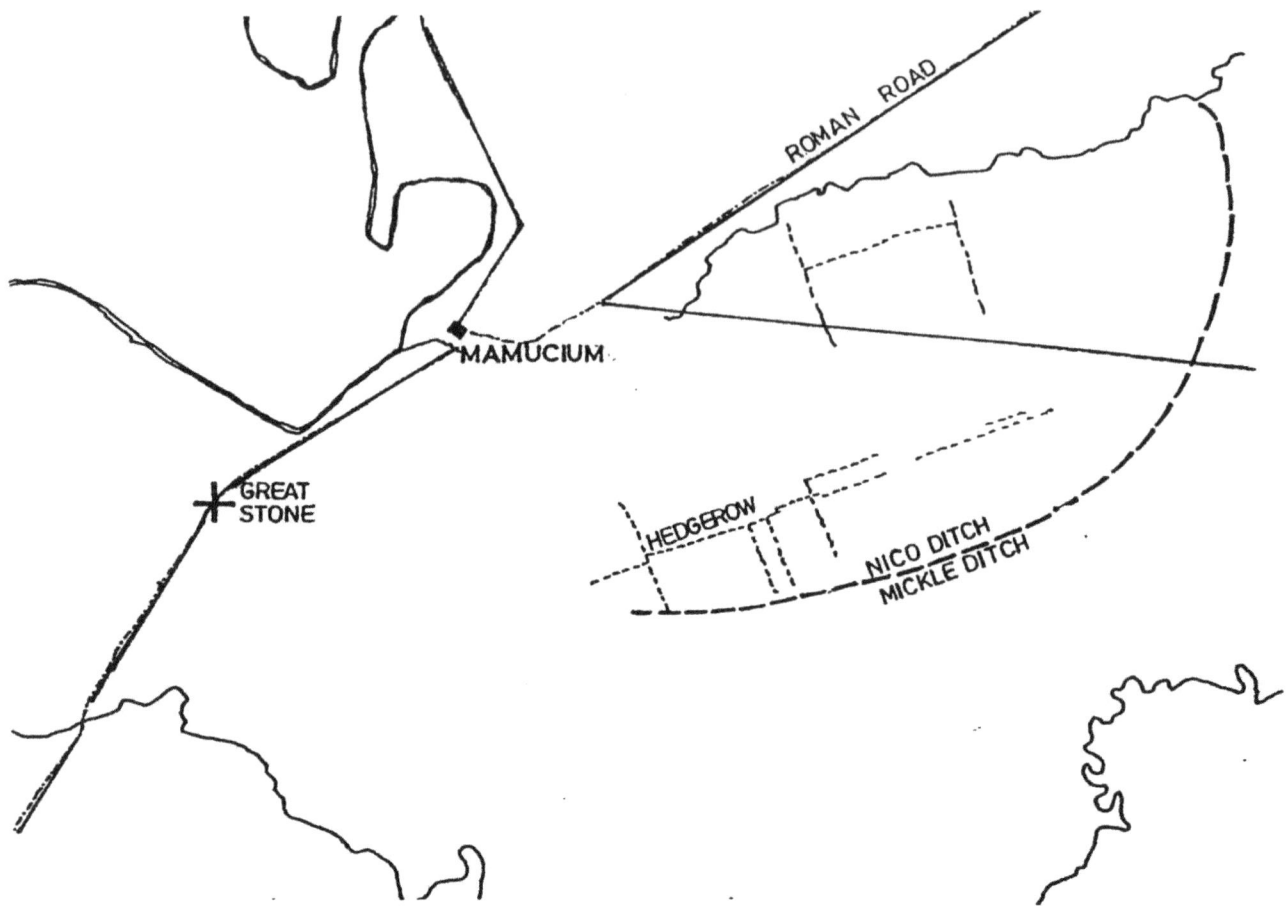

Fig. 6.1 Manchester: the Mickle Ditch, Roman roads and the hedgerow line

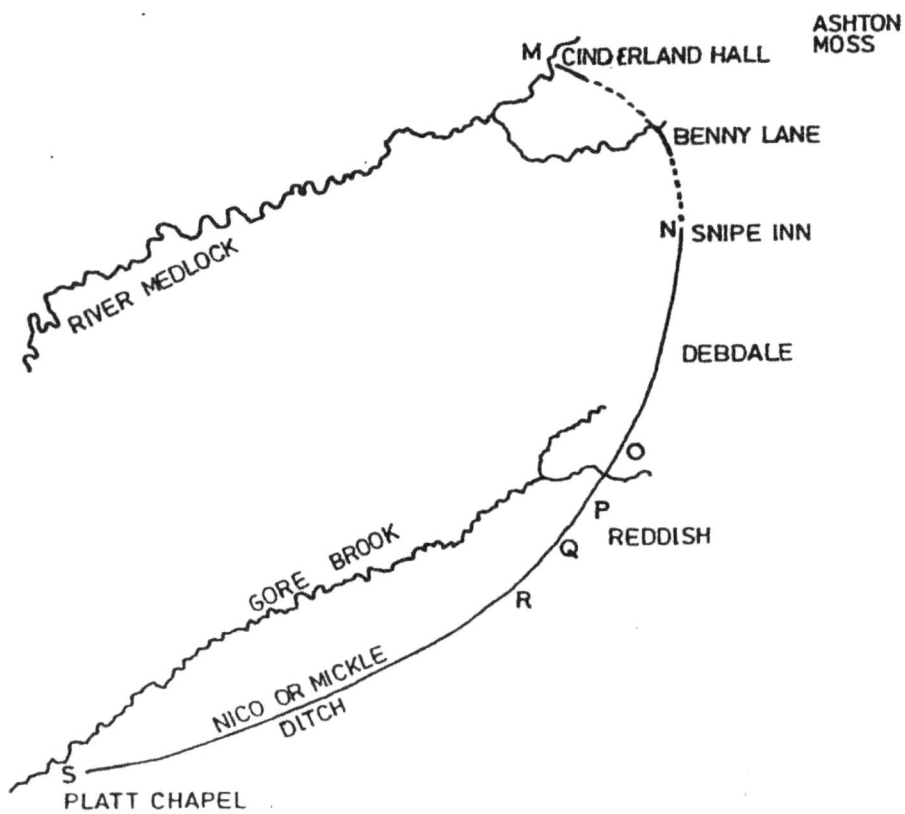

Fig. 6.2 The geometric points of the Mickle Ditch

The geometry of the ditch line
The ditch line follows the line MNOPQRS. (See Figure. 6.2)

Beginning at the NE, the ditch approximates very closely to three arcs of circles and three straight alignments, two of which are tangential to the arcs. See Figure. 6.3.

A. Three arcs of circles.
  i. MN is the arc of a circle (a) whose centre is Y and whose radius is YN = 45 *actus*.
  ii. NO is the arc of a circle (b) whose centre is X and whose radius is XN = 120 *actus*.
  iii. PQ is an arc of a circle (c) whose centre is Z and whose radius is ZQ = 75 *actus*.

Note that 75 + 45 = 120.

B. Two tangents.
  i. OP is 16 *actus* long and is a tangent to circle (b) at O connecting to point P on circle (c).
  ii. QR is 25 *actus* long and is a tangent to circle (c) at Q.

C. The last section from R to S is 56.66 *actus* and is a chord so shallow as to be almost straight, save for the last couple of hundred feet, which turn slightly northwards.

D. XN = XF = 120 *actus*, so the triangle XNF is isosceles.
E. FQ is five *actus*.
F. SQ = QN = 117 *actus* and NM is half of this, 58.5 *actus*.

It looks as though the original design for the eastern part of the ditch was the conjunction of three arcs of circles whose centres were on two sides of a 120 *actus* equilateral triangle. But this appears to have been modified into an isosceles triangle by extending one side to 125 *actus*. The 120 *actus* sides were divided, for the purpose of forming the circles, at 75 and 45, since 45 + 74 = 120. But the modified model shifted the centre of the third circle (Z) five *actus* along the long side of the isosceles triangle making the line of the ditch swing further south and requiring the two arcs to be joined by short tangent of 16 *actus*. The effect of this manoeuvre, no doubt intentional, was to shift the line of the ditch further southwards, so that instead of running close to the course of the Gore Brook, it ran across the flat the watershed of the Gore and Fallowfield Brooks.

Lay out method
Arcs of circles of 5,400 feet (45 *actus*) and 9,000 feet (75 *actus*) radius would not have been laid out using huge ropes, but by applying the theorem of the equality of angles in the same segment of a circle. The SW end of the ditch would have been visible from Ashton Moss and having decided the three main alignments, the surveyors would have knocked in posts at the end of each. To connect each end by an arc, thus making each alignment into a chord, they would first have decided the perpendicular distance between the midpoint of the chord and that of the arc. Then going to that point they would have installed the *groma* and adjusted its arms to align on the marker posts at each end of the chord and by moving towards each in turn, but always keeping each marker in the *groma* sights, they would trace out an arc that would have been marked by pegs as they progressed.The radii of the circles, 45, 75 and 120 *actus* indicates that the surveyors worked to a carefully drafted plan. The inescapable conclusion is that the Mickle Ditch was laid out *after* a careful survey of the whole area and is thus a Roman work. The question arises as to why the equilateral triangle was made isosceles so as to shift the line of the ditch southwards and in turn this raises the question of the ditch's function.

Relationship of the Mickle Ditch to the centuriation
Figure 6.4 shows the ditch in relation to the centuriation. The solid grid lines west and north of the ditch are those of the putative grid already described. The broken grid lines east and south of the southern *limes* are the projected lines of that grid. There are six points at which the ditch impinges upon the half-century projected grid line intersections. At the most easterly ditch section (Benny Lane) the putative grid line makes a perfect tangent to the ditch line on the arc of circle (a). This is unlikely to have been accidental.

This arrangement immediately suggests that the centuriation may have extended south and east of the ditch, in which case the ditch may not have formed a boundary at all but rather had a drainage function. The land over which it runs is heavy clay and is almost flat, though it does slope very gently SW. Figure 6.4 shows the point heights marked on the 1848 map. The land to the east of ditch is higher as far as the watershed of the R. Tame.   North of the Snipe Inn, it slopes slightly (326 to 321 feet OD) towards Bell Clough, and to the south and west it falls to 300 feet OD at Audenshaw village and 279 feet OD beyond Fallowfield Brook. It is significant that the western section of the ditch ran through a tract of former wetland to terminate at the aptly named *Rushholme*. The ditch's curved course between Ashton Moss and Debdale can now be seen as following a crescent shaped piece of almost flat, clay land that would have been wet and sour before drainage. The ditch leads water out of the Moss to the SW, while the section at Benny Lane drained into Lumb Clough and that by Cinderland Hall into the R. dlock. The ditch section between Debdale and Platt Chapel drains the flat ground between the parallel, westward flowing Gore and Fallowfield brooks.

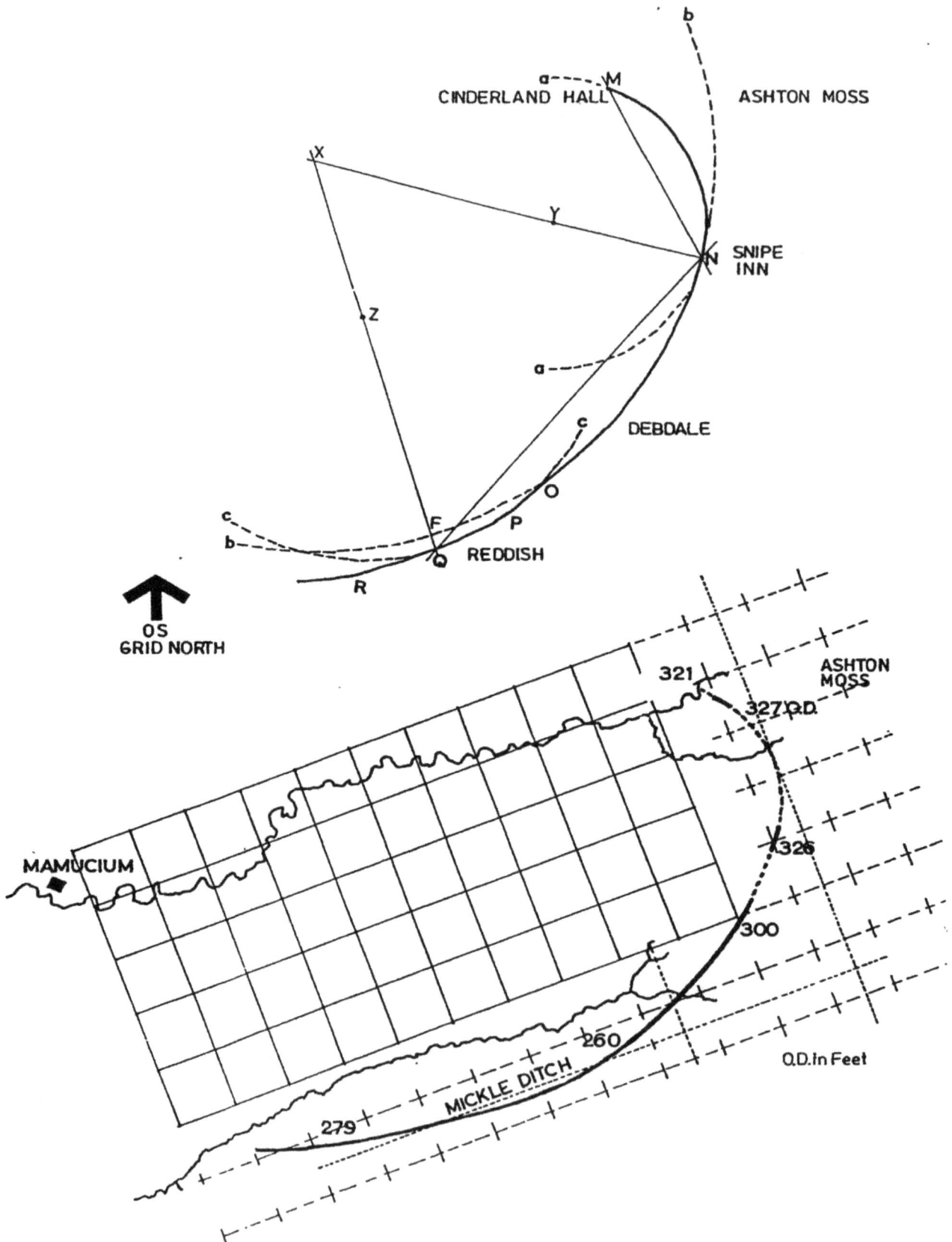

CINDERLAND HALL

ASHTON MOSS

SNIPE INN

DEBDALE

REDDISH

OS
GRID NORTH

321

ASHTON MOSS

327 O.D.

326

300

MAMUCIUM

260

MICKLE DITCH

279

O.D. in Feet

Fig. 6.3   (Above) The Mickle Ditch: Geometry of the sections

Fig. 6.4   (Below) The Mickle Ditch and the centuriation
(Figures are feet OD)

Mr Richard Bellhouse, a noted Roman archaeologist and former land drainage expert, considers such a ditch would have provided very effective drainage. On flat ground, water will flow out of each end of a ditch, and one six to ten feet deep could conduct a considerable volume (Bellhouse, pers. comm.). It may be that the apparently missing sections on the most north-westerly arc were never dug at all.

Discussion

To summarise, the Mickle Ditch was laid out as series of conjoined arcs and tangents whose dimensions were defined in the standard Roman *agrimensorial* unit, the *actus* and the only practical method of doing it required the use of Euclidian geometry. Since the ditch formed the boundary to several Anglo-Saxon manors, it must be Roman. The ditch fits neatly into, and probably postdates the centuriation, which probably extended south and east. In such a case, it is unlikely to have been a boundary and was probably for drainage.

There is one further point to reflect upon and that is as to *why* such a curiously geometric ditch line was laid out. The approach was not simply utilitarian, as would have been that of a modern engineer who would have cut several straight ditch alignments that would serve equally well as drains. Again we suggest that it was drawn in accordance with Pythagorean notions of mathematical harmony intended to invite divine approval, for the geometry of the line is not apparent from the ground.

****

PART SEVEN

THE FRONTIER WALLS

The two northern walls appear to have been planned from the map. The clues lie in the latitudinal and longitudinal distances between the forts, which were analysed using a spreadsheet. The forts were listed in the first spreadsheet column and their five figure OS grid references in the second (eastings) and third (northings). These references were taken carefully with a scale rule at the centre of the fort, as shown on the relevant special edition OS maps; the Antonine Wall (1969) and Hadrian's Wall (1972). The remaining columns displayed the distances in *actus* and *centuriae*, of, a) the NS and EW distances of each fort from a separate datum point whose OS reference could be inserted at will; b) the actual NS and EW distances between each fort.

The Antonine Wall will be considered first because its underlying grid plan is more evident.

Antonine Wall
The forts and their OS grid references are listed in Table 7.1 and their disposition shown in Figure 7.1. The most easterly fort, Carriden, lies 1,594 *actus*, east of Old Kilpatrick, the most westerly. Given the limitations imposed by the map scale, this EW distance approximates 1,600 *actus*. The most northerly fort, Carriden is 259 *actus* north of the most southerly, Balmuidy. Again, allowing for reasonable error, the dimension is probably 260 *actus*. The Wall is therefore contained within a grid 1,600 by 260 *actus*, or 80 x 13 *centuriae*. In miles the distances are 38.25 EW and 6.25 NS.

Table 7.1
EW distances between Antonine Wall forts in relation to the Carrickstone.

Distances in *actus*; *centuriae* in brackets; whole numbers of *centuriae* in bold type

Fort	OS reference		From the Carrickstone		Between forts E to W	
Old Kilpatrick	246.00	673.10	W	830	(41.5)		
Duntocher	249.52	672.63	W	730	(36.5)	99	**(5.0)**
Castle Hill	252.45	672.63	W	648	(32.4)	83	(4.1)
New Kilpatrick	254.56	672.08	W	588	(29.4)	60	**(3.0)**
Balmuidy	258.11	671.70	W	488	(24.4)	100	**(5.0)**
Cadder	261.68	672.55	W	388	(19.4)	100	**(5.0)**
Kirkintiloch	265.20	673.96	W	289	(14.4)	99	**(5.0)**
Auchendavy	267.73	674.93	W	217	(10.9)	71	(3.6)
Bar Hill	270.73	675.90	W	133	(6.6)	85	(4.2)
Croy Hill	273.35	676.53	W	59	(2.9)	74	(3.7)
Carrickstone	275.475	676.100	-			-	
Westerwood	276.08	677.23	E	18	(0.9)	77	(3.8)
Castlecary	278.95	678.25	E	99	(4.9)	81	(4.1)
Seabegs	281.83	679.53	E	180	(9.0)	81	(4.1)
Rough Castle	284.35	679.85	E	251	(12.6)	71	(3.6)
Camelon	286.35	680.95	E	307	(15.4)	56	(2.8)
Falkirk	288.18	679.93	E	359	(17.9)	51	(2.6)
Mumrills	291.85	679.31	E	462	(23.1)	104	(5.2)
Inveravon	295.15	679.56	E	555	(27.8)	93	(4.6)
Kinniel	298.30	680.50	E	644	(32.2)	89	(4.4)
Bridgeness	301.30	681.35	E	729	(36.4)	85	(4.2)
Carriden	302.60	680.75	E	764	(38.2)	36	(1.8)

The centre of this grid is the point where the half way easting and the half way northing intersect at 274.29E 676.45N, on a hill just north of Cumbernauld south of the Croy Hill and Westerwood forts. It is very close to a now filled-in well in a small fir plantation at Muirhead Farm (OS 275.44E 676.8N). On the same meridian, 20 *actus* to the south, and upon a hilltop next to a modern trig point stands the *Carrickstone* (OS 275.48E 676.10N).

According to the plate attached to the railings around the Carrickstone, it is a second century Roman altar of unknown provenance. Because of its name, tradition has associated it with Robert the Bruce, (Earl of Carrick) in whose honour it was presumed to have been taken from a nearby Wall fort. Until recently it stood upon an open site commanding fine views in all

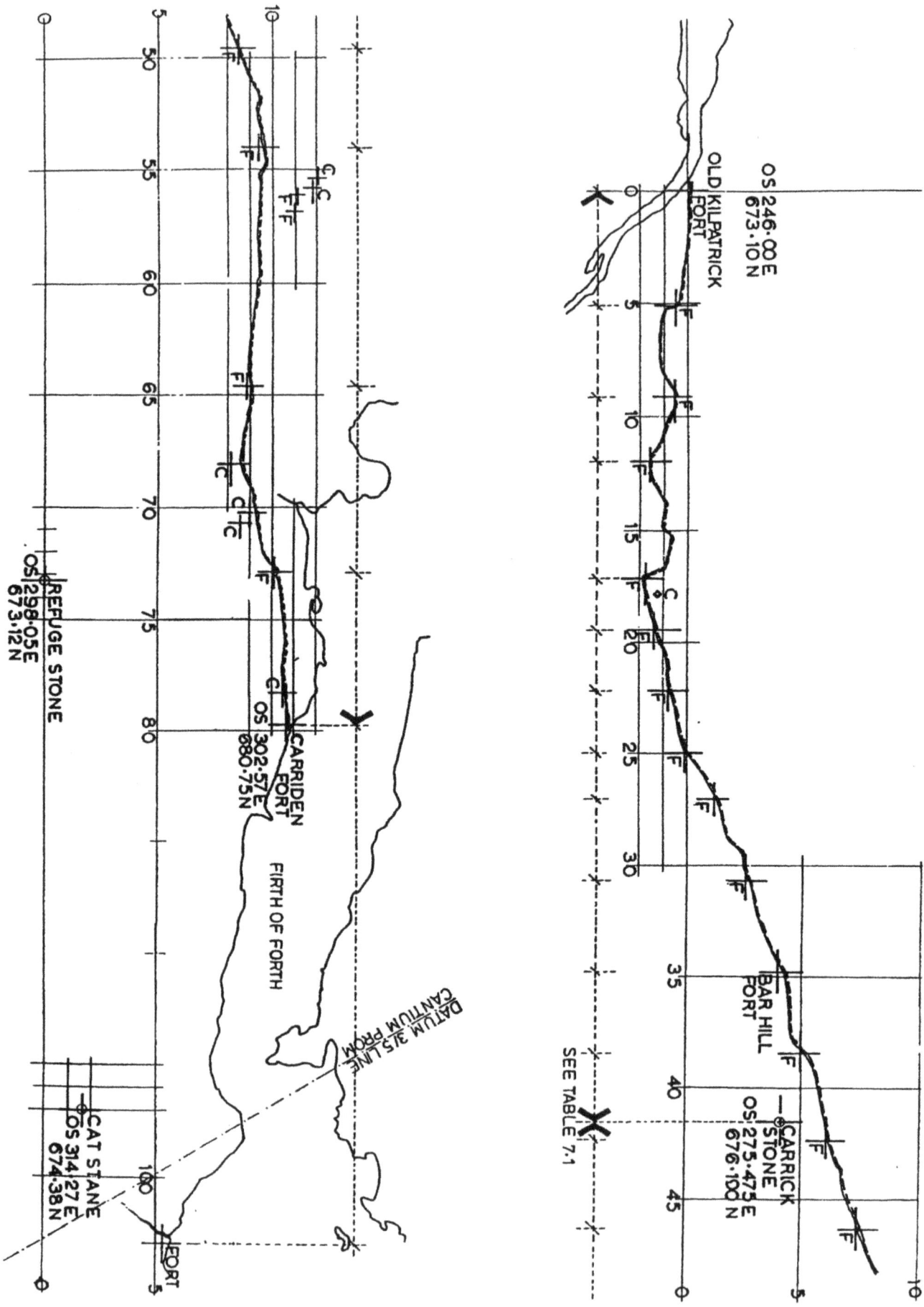

Fig. 7.1 The Antonine Wall

(This diagram puts the EW datum at the latitude of Old Kilpatrick. The probable true datum of the whole system is 5 *centuriae* N, through the Muirhead well. Note that the line *Atan* 3/5 W of N from *Cantium Prom* cuts this line, 100 *centuriae* E of Old Kilpatrick.)

commanding fine views in all directions but a housing development has now obscured these, though the Firth of Forth and the Pentland Hills are still visible. Its location, by a modern trig point, is quite significant and consistent with its marking a Roman survey point.

The Carrickstone is 43.9 (44) miles west and 209.6 (210) miles north of Chester, and 360.2 (360) miles north and 243.9 (244) miles west of *Cantium Prom*. It is also 74.9 (75) miles north of the mean line of Hadrian's Wall (see below). On the Eratosthenes model, this distance is 1° and from *Cantium Prom* the Carrickstone is 4 4/5 ° N. See Table 7.2.

Table 7.2
Distances of Carrickstone and Hadrian's Wall from *Cantium Prom*

Site	OS grid reference	Distance from Cantium Prom		
		west		*north*
Cantium Prom	636.10E 143.30N	-		-
Hadrian's Wall	Mean 565.12N	-		285.26 miles
Carrickstone	275.47E 676.10N	243.9 miles		360.20 miles
NS distance from Hadrian's Wall to Carrickstone				74.94 miles

The true centre of the grid could be the well at Muirhead Farm, which raises the possibility of an ancient shrine, perhaps that of the presiding deity of the Wall and possibly the *Medio Nemeton* of the Ravenna Cosmography (MacDonald 1934, 189). The well is at the top of a very wet field (muir) and the farmer remembers it as a stone-lined well now lost in the undergrowth of a new plantation. Its location on the northern slope would preclude its use as a surveying point, which would have been better placed on the hilltop at one standard surveying unit (20 *actus*) southwards. It is, of course, possible that the well has no connection with the Carrickstone.

The spacing of the seven forts between Old Kilpatrick and Kirkintiloch strongly suggests that they were intended to be five *centuriae* apart (Table 7.1, column 4). This, together with the other evidence, suggests that the ground over which the wall was built was first surveyed from a datum point (Carrickstone) related to the Roman "national" grid.

Hadrian's Wall

The OS references of the Hadrian's Wall forts are listed in Table 7.3, together with the distances of each from either end. The inter-fort distances are also given.

The mean northing of the forts is OS 565.12N; 285.3 miles north of *Cantium Prom* and 134.5 miles north of Chester. It is likely the Romans intended the mean EW line to be 135 miles north of Chester and 285 miles from *Cantium Prom*. The 135-mile distance is 1 4/5° (Eratosthenes) north of Chester and 3 4/5° north of *Cantium Prom*. See Figure 7.2.

The mean easting of the forts is OS 375.94E. This is 175.94 (say 176.0) miles west of *Cantium Prom* and 24.1 (say 24) miles east of Chester. The sum of the EW distances (the *Cantium Prom* to Chester dimension) is 200 miles (176 + 24 = 200). The centre datum is therefore OS 375.94E 565.11N. In miles, the inclination from *Cantium Prom* is *Atan* 176/285, or 0.61. This is very close to 3/5 (0.6). The nearest fort is Housesteads (OS 378.96E), which is exactly 287.8 miles (599.3 *centuriae*) north and 173.9 miles (362.2 *centuriae*) west of *Cantium Prom*. It bears *Atan* 173.9 / 287.8 = 0.6, or 3/5 W of N from *Cantium Prom*. Table 7.3 shows that Bowness is exactly 80.0 *centuriae* west of Housesteads and Wallsend is exactly 72 *centuriae* east. Another 8 *centuriae* east stands South Shields fort. It more than likely, therefore, that Housesteads stands at, or very close to, the centre datum for the whole wall.

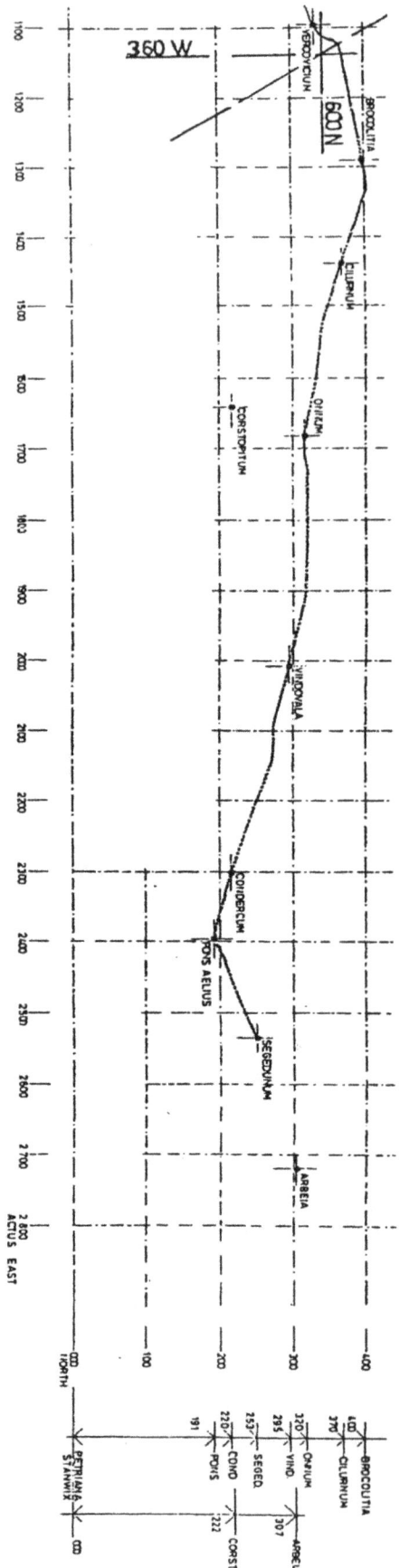

HADRIAN'S WALL

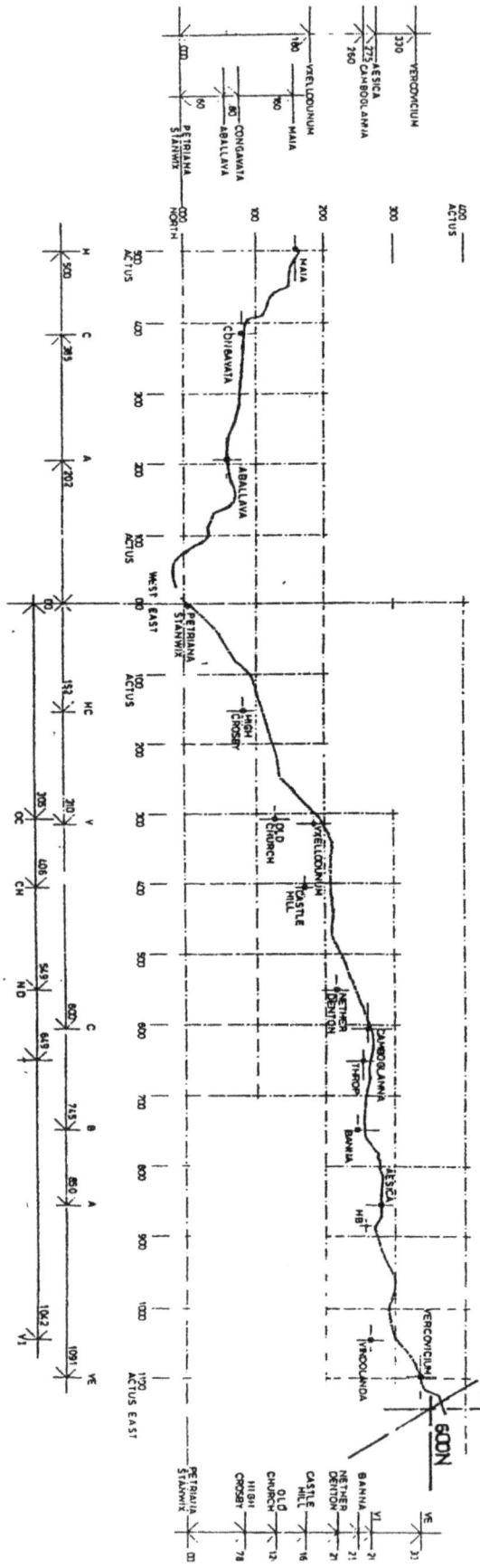

Fig. 7.2 Hadrian's Wall

(This diagram puts the EW datum at Stanwix but the true datum may have been near Housesteads on a alignment Atan 3/5 W of N from *Cantium Prom.*)

Table 7.3
EW distances of forts of Hadrian's Wall forts from both ends
Distances in *centuriae*: whole numbers in bold type

Fort	Grid references		Dimensions in centuriae		
			W to E	*E to W*	*Inter-fort distances*
Bowness	322.25	562.68	-	151.8	
Drumburgh	326.50	559.83	-6.0	145.8	6.0
Burgh by Sands	332.90	559.15	-15.0	136.8	9.0
Stanwix	340.22	557.14	-25.3	126.5	10.3
Castlesteads	351.70	563.46	-41.5	110.3	16.2
Birdoswald	361.56	566.28	-55.3	96.4	13.9
Carvoran	366.53	565.72	-62.3	89.4	7.0
Gt. Chesters	370.37	566.78	-67.7	84.0	5.4
Housesteads	378.96	568.81	-79.8	71.9	12.1
Carrawborough	385.90	571.18	-89.6	62.2	9.8
Chesters	391.17	570.17	-97.0	54.7	7.4
Halton Chesters	399.72	568.47	-109.1	42.7	12.0
Rudchester	411.25	567.56	-125.3	26.5	16.2
Benwell	421.56	564.78	-139.8	12.0	14.5
Newcastle	425.07	563.84	-144.7	7.0	4.9
Wallsend	430.06	566.06	-151.8	-	7.0
Means	375.98	565.12			

The westernmost fort, Bowness is 212.4 miles west of *Cantium Prom* and 133 miles north of Chester. Wallsend is 139.4 miles west of *Cantium Prom* and 60.5 miles east of Chester. From these data, the Wall's EW dimension is 72.98 (73) miles, or 3435 *actus*, or 151.8 *centuriae*. From the Chester datum it is exactly 73 miles, 3041.66 *actus* or 152.0 *centuriae*. The discrepancy is negligible.

Interrelationship of the walls
Table 7.4 shows the distances from *Cantium Prom* and Chester to the centre datum point of Hadrian's Wall and the Carrickstone. The Carrickstone is 75 miles north of the centre datum point of Hadrian's W and 67.9 (68) miles to the east. It is therefore *Atan* 11/10 W of N (75/68 = 1.1).

Table 7.4
Distances between the Carrickstone (C) and the centre datum of Hadrian's Wall (H)
(In miles from Chester and *Cantium Prom*:)

		North		East and West	
	H		C	H	C
Cantium Prom	285.3		360.2	176.0	243.9
Differences		74.9		67.9	
Chester	134.5		209.6	24.0	43.9
Differences		75.1		67.9	
Differences	150.8		150.6	200.0	200.0
Means		75.0		67.9	

Discussion
In the siting and lay out of such important military structures as frontier walls one would not expect to detect a perverse addiction to sacred geometry cutting across the imperatives of defence. Nor do we. Nevertheless, there are

certain features in both defensive systems that seem all of a piece with what we have discovered elsewhere. The mean EW line of the Antonine Wall is 75 miles (1° Eratosthenes) north of the mean line of Hadrian's Wall, and Housesteads stands *Atan* 3/5 W of N from *Cantium Prom*. The mid EW point of Hadrian's Wall is 176.0 miles from *Cantium Prom* and 24.0 miles from Chester. In terms of latitudes on the model of Eratosthenes, the mean latitude of Hadrian's Wall is 3 4/5° north and the Antonine Wall 4 4/5° north of *Cantium Prom*. The whole picture is consistent with the map grid having been used in planning the frontiers.

****

PART EIGHT

A NEW CRITERION FOR ROMAN ROADS

The proposed Roman grid may be drawn upon the Ordnance Survey map using the eastings and northings at 10 or 20 Roman mile intervals from *Cantium Prom* as shown in Appendix 10. On the 1:25.000 map, one mile is 59.2 mm, one *centuria* (2,400 feet) is 28.4 mm. It is almost certain that further studies of the Roman British landscape made with a map bearing this grid will reveal hitherto unsuspected Roman features and shed new light on recognised ones. For example, road lines that are suspected of being Roman but for which there is slight supporting evidence. Three examples from Cumberland illustrate the point.

Roman Roads at Carlisle
Three major roads approaching the Roman city are aligned on the cardinal points of the compass, a common Roman practice derived from Greek precedents (Dilke 1971, 86-87).

From the North: Scotland Road, whose Roman precursor ran about 50 metres west of the modern road (Hogg 1952, Caruanna and Coulston 1987).
From the West: Burgh Road, probably overlying the last section of the Roman road from the Kirkbride fort (Bellhouse 1982).
From the East: Warwick Road.
From the South: Botchergate enters the Roman city at an angle because the line due south is occupied by the River Caldew. The projected alignments of these roads meet at OS 399.4E 558.8N, a point just SW of the cathedral. See Figure 8.1.

Castrigg to Castlesteads on Hadrian's Wall (Appleby Street)
There is a putative 30-mile Roman road along the eastern side of the Eden valley, apparently connecting Castlesteads Wall fort (OS 351.50E 563.50N) with the Brougham – Brough road (A66) at Castrigg (OS 368.15E 521.55N) (Richardson 1984). The clues to its Roman origin are few but significant. Its mean course is *Atan* 2/5 W of N.

Dalston to Hayton
Another putative Roman route runs south of Carlisle, between Dalston and Hayton, part of it along the Newbiggin Road mentioned in respect of the Inglewood centuriation. It has long puzzled local antiquarians but always defied explanation. It has four straight alignments between Pow Bank and Low Gelt Bridge and each node fits the NSEW grid that includes Wall Knowe. The alignments therefore subtend angles with tangents of rational fractions to the grid. See Figure 8.2, which shows a reconstructed Roman map of the Carlisle district. In detail, the alignments are as follows.

1. From Green Lane, Pow Bank (338.49E 550.15N), at the northern end of an Inglewood *limes,* the modern road runs to Oak Dene (339.75E 550.95N), 30 *actus* (20 x 1.5) west and 180 *actus* (20 x 9) south of Wall Knowe. It is aligned *Atan* 3/5 N of E.
2. It then becomes Newbiggin Road due east for almost 100 *actus*, (20 x 5) to Newbiggin Hall (343.42E 551.00N).
3. The line then shifts *Atan* 3/4 N of E along the line of a pre-motorway road that crossed the Roman Carlisle-Brougham road (A6) and then closely accompanies the road through Cumwhinton to Wetheral Abbey, where it crosses the R. Eden by an ancient ford. It then goes along the main street of Great Corby, much of it a hollow-way, and at the end of that village by a short disused lane to a footpath to a hamlet (334.46E 555.22N) significantly named *Broadwath* (broad ford) in 1285 (Armstrong *et al*, undated, 161). Broadwath is 60 *actus* (20 x 3) south, and 220 *actus* (20 x 11) east, of Wall Knowe.
4. The line then shifts again, (*Atan* 6/5 N of E) along the road to How Street (349.90E 557.00N) ten *actus* south of Wall Knowe. There is a one-km. gap across the fields before Hayton, beyond which the line coincides with the road to Low Gelt Bridge, 320 *actus* (20 x 16) *centuriae* east and 2.5 *centuriae* north of Wall Knowe. The alignment may then be projected to the *Stanegate* NW of Brampton and to the Wall at Haytongate (355.40E 564.60N) above Lanercost Bridge. *Haytongate* was formerly *Aikton Gate,* so the hint of a road to Hayton is unfounded (Armstrong *et al* undated), unless at some remote period it followed the route given here to Newbiggin Road and then along northing 550.95 to Aikton, near Thursby.

Almost the whole distance from Pow Bank to Low Gelt Bridge coincides with, or is shadowed closely by, modern road. The only gaps are a field at Wetheral and the one km. between Toppin Castle and Hayton village. The route is shown on Hodgkinson and Donald's map (*circa* 1775) where the central part of Newbiggin Road was missing, though each end is shown. The same map shows the road from Great Corby to Broadwath following what is now the footpath. Another map of 1704 indicates that between the Hayton boundary and How Street, it had already formed the base line for enclosures (Graham 1907). In summary, this undoubtedly very old route neatly fits the grid, shifting alignment at its *centuria* intersections but otherwise is largely devoid of the usual clues to a Roman origin.

69

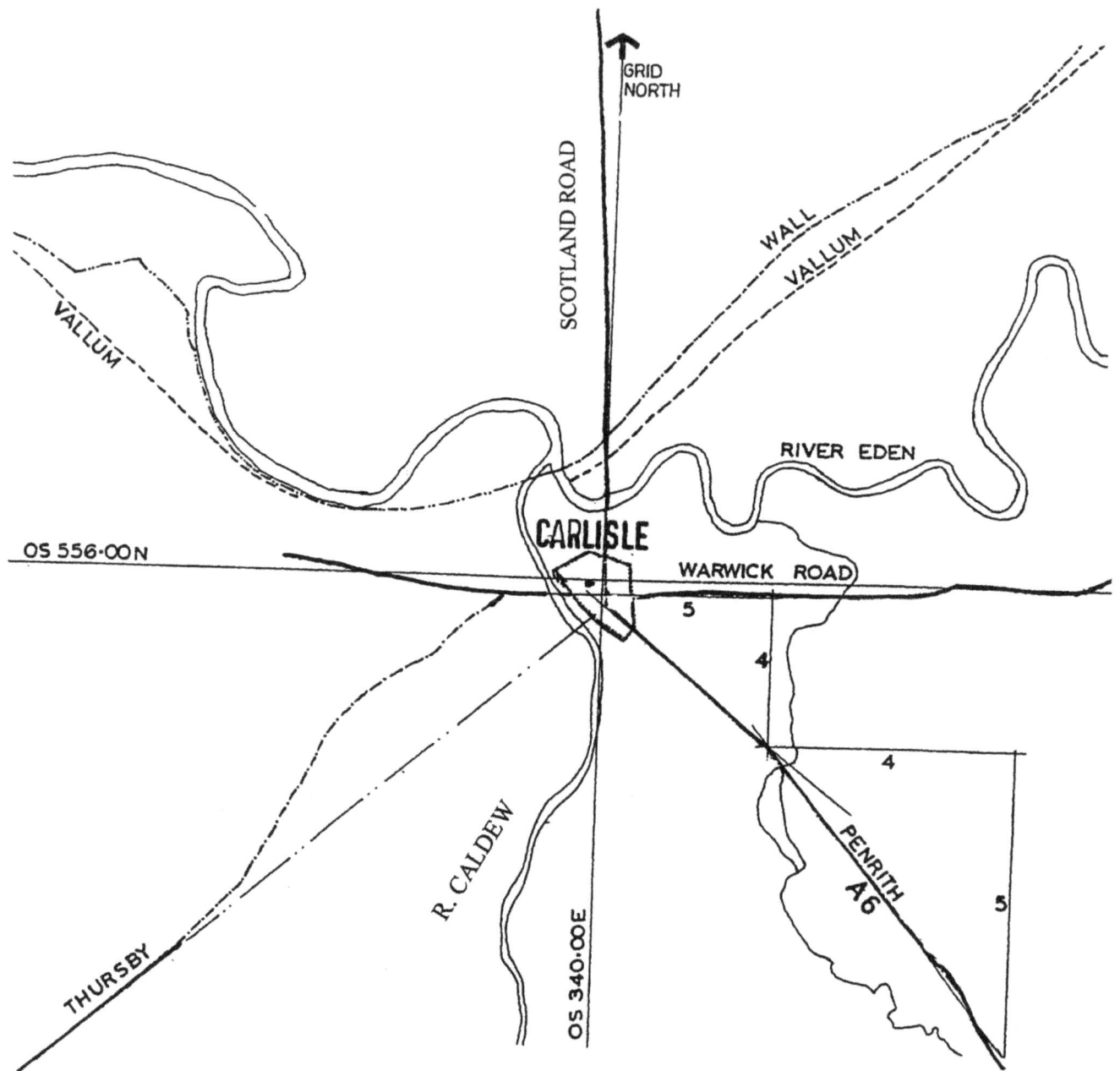

Fig 8.1 Roman roads on the cardinal points approaching Carlisle

(The approach from the south was compromised by the River Petteril.)
(Note the alignment inclinations of the road to the south)

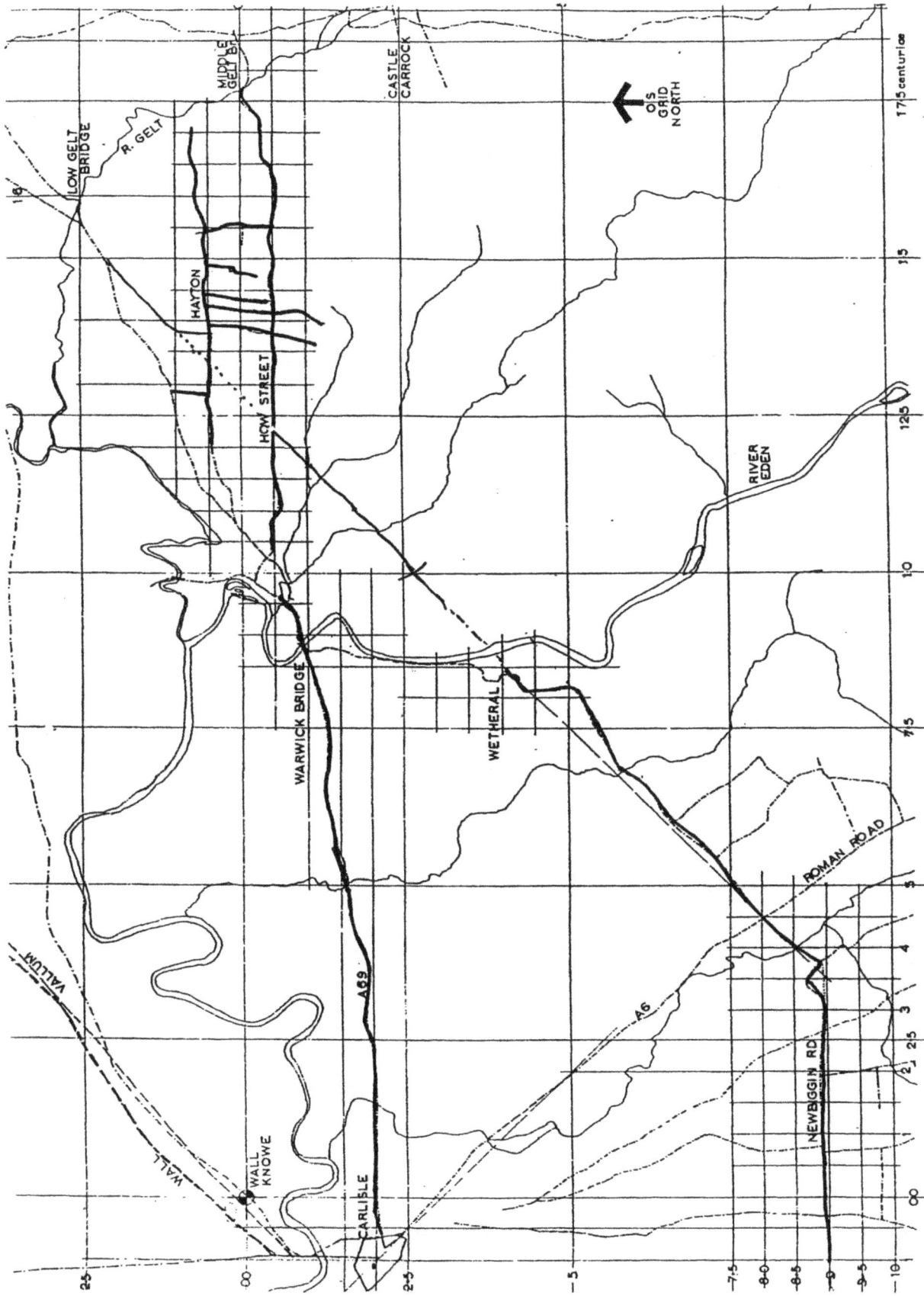

Fig 8.2 NSEW grid S and E of Carlisle
(Note probable centuriation at Hayton and Newbiggin Rd – Low Gelt Bridge line.)

71

PART NINE

GENERAL DISCUSSION

It is first necessary to consider the accuracy of our methods. The data we have used may be verified from the OS maps and an impartial worker repeating our studies will obtain similar results, though he may dispute our conclusions. The OS grid references have been expressed as five digit values from the OS base lines such that the fifth digit defines tens of metres. Given the variables inherent in surveys and map-making, especially with roads being shown many times wider than they could possibly be, every value should be understood to be a best estimate and nothing more. Moreover, any Roman survey would be subject to some variation.

We have put forward evidence and arguments, which even if they do not convince the reader, at least form the basis of a hypothesis that may be tested by future observations. We believe that further study will reveal that much of Britain was surveyed and planned according to the outlines given here.

To summarise the argument, the mean lines of certain Roman roads in the east and the west of the country are aligned to OS grid N, not the local true N, by angles with tangents of simple rational fractions. Therefore the ground must first have been surveyed and a scale map drawn with a grid orientated like the OS grid. Roads were aligned so that they *tended* to run from one grid-line intersection to another, thus forming hypotenuses to right-angled triangles whose non-hypotenuse sides are in whole number ratios.

The Romans almost certainly began surveying Britain immediately after coming ashore. They came primed with the latest academic works as well as with local intelligence from spies and traders. They were fully conversant with the techniques of map-making and their first objective was to establish survey base lines in the south. The Foss Way was probably laid out immediately after the establishment of the mid longitude and then may have served as a datum line for the districts it traversed. Thereafter, the survey could have been extended in corridors along other lines of communication, if necessary skirting large upland areas, but in time covering the whole country. The same map was used to plan centuriation systems where the *limites* were aligned to take account of land relief, though probably set out from the main roads.

But the map, with its NSEW grid, appears to have been used by planners in a way that might strike us as bizarre, but which undoubtedly conformed to the Pythagorean view of the world. This was to dispose towns and forts in such a way that they related spatially to each other by certain triangles, especially the 3/5 right angled triangle, and at the same time were separated by distances that were multiples of squares on the hypotenuses of such triangles. Indeed there is reason to believe that the planners went so far as to superimpose upon the surveyors' NSEW map grid, other grids that were angled *Atan* 3/5 to it. In so doing they were probably exercising a priestly function to ensure that the outcome was pleasing to the gods.

At first sight the initial survey would seem to be a stupendous task but it would have merely entailed knocking in posts along lines carefully set out with *gromae* and sundials. The whole survey south of Humber Mersey line could have been done in months, given adequate manpower, and there is not the slightest reason for doubting the Roman capacity to do it. Compared to the labour about to be expended in road and fort construction, the effort was trivial.

It is likely that the original Roman map was made in sections, although a map of the whole province may have been prepared at some point. Whether these were on papyrus or some other medium cannot be known, but certainly they must have perished within a few hundred years. Some may have been copied and survived, perhaps sadly corrupted, into the mediaeval period. Certainly, Bede knew that the earth was spherical and appeared to have had fairly accurate ideas about its surface (Beazley, undated). Since he never left the north of England his knowledge must have been derived from the fine monastic libraries at Wearmouth and Jarrow where he spent his days (Mayer-Harting 1977, 40). It is highly probable that such libraries retained copies of maps as well as ancient geographic texts. One wonders whether the Doomsday officials had some sort of map to hand because they frequently described features in terms of length and breadth in a way that is meaningless without some sort of sketch or some notion of orientation. An enquiry into this matter might yield interesting results.

We suspect that the sectional map of Britain was available to Ptolemy but the co-ordinates that he abstracted from it became horribly corrupted in the following millennium. It is simply not believable that the Romans planned and governed Britain with nothing better than the map known to us from the mediaeval copy of his work.

The suggestion that the 17 *actus centuria* was customary in the south of Britain, though based on data that some might be reluctant to accept, namely the distribution of villa sites on *Atan* 3/5 planning grids, nevertheless affords a plausible explanation of the origin of our statute measures. The idea is also consistent with the notion that the great ox plough was already in use in those parts during the Roman period. To be worked effectively, this revolutionary machine required a long furrow because it could not be turned round in a short distance.

It is likely that some Roman survey cairns have survived intact, though without any identifying feature to proclaim their origin they have not been recognised. Only the Carrickstone appears to have survived with its provenance intact but others may await recognition. It is likely that survey beacons marked with dedicatory inscriptions to pagan gods were overthrown and replaced with Christian crosses and this, we suspect, accounts for many such monuments being found in remote places. Again, further work is needed.

The major obstacle to accepting the idea of a Roman map of the sophistication that we have proposed lies in the absence of any detailed description of such a thing in the ancient literature. It is, at first sight, surprising that despite mentions of maps in the *Corpus Agrimensorum* and the discussion of map projections and concern for accuracy found in Ptolemy, so many scholars seem to dismiss the very notion that good Roman maps, as opposed to simple itineries, ever existed. There are at least two probable reasons for this.

One reason, if we are correct in our suppositions about the priestly use of oblique map grids, is that the Christians saw such devices primarily as objects of pagan practice and expunged them from the mind of man. To this undoubtedly was added the ancient patrician prejudice against the application of mathematics and science to practical ends. Writing of Francis Bacon, the founder of modern natural philosophy, Macaulay commented on the classical view that mathematics was degraded by its practical application. Plato, he noted, referred to the "vulgar crowd of geometricians." Geometry was, literally, measuring the earth, so the aristocratic view of *agrimensores* could not be clearer. "The office of geometry", according to Plato, "was to discipline the mind, not to minister to the base wants of the body." The Church maintained this prejudice throughout the following centuries and despite Bacon's efforts and the achievements of modern science, the notion that science and technology are not for gentlemen still survives.

****

APPENDICES

Appendix 1: OS grid references of Foss Way alignment nodes
Lincoln cathedral 49770 37170: Bracebridge 49700 36885: Potter Hill 48560 36055: East Stoke 47520 34928: Saxondale 46870 33970: Cotgrave Gorse 46590 33470: Six Hills 46435 32080: Leicester Nth 45900 30530: Leicester W End 45750 30340: High Cross 44730 28860: Bretford Sth 44295 27645: Halford Nth 42635 24615: Portobello Fm 42330 23985: Moreton in Marsh 42070 23360: Stow on Wold 41900 24425: Northleach 41100 21490: Fosse Cross Sth 40630 20865: Ampney Downs 40465 20710: Ragged Hedge 40390 20485: Cirencester 40230 20200: Kemble Airfield 39605 19690: Merchants Fm 39170 19100: Nettleton Scrub 38265 17750: Collerone Airfield 38015 17300: Banner Down 37925 16815: Fortnight Farm 37250 16100: Ashgrove Cemetery 37080 15785: Clandon 36840 15590: Killing Knap 36620 15175: Oakhill 36415 14740: Little Pennard 36155 13745: Wraxall Nth 36035 13680: Cary Fitzpaine 35450 12760: Ilchester 35200 12245: Ringwell Hill 34640 11760: Lopen Head 34240 11470: Dinnington 34015 11300: Tytherleigh 33185 10350: Axminster 33010 09840:

Appendix 2: To convert distances in km. to Roman measure.
To convert distances in km. to Roman measure, multiply by 1000 and again by 39.36; then divide by 11.65 to give Roman feet. To change this to Roman miles, divide by 5000. To change feet to *actus*, divide by 120. So, km. x 28.2 = *actus*.

Appendix 3: To convert *actus* to km.
To convert *actus* to km., multiply by 120 to give feet and then again by 11.65 to give inches. Then divide by 39.36 to give metres and again by 1000 to give km. So *actus* x 0.03555 = km.

Appendix 4 Alignment nodes on the Low Borrowbridge to Carlisle road:
Alignment 1. Low Borrowbridge 36095 50130: Roundthwaite North 36100 501420: Howenook Pike 35990 51007: Ewe Close 36095 51365: Reagill 36081 51709: *Alignment 2.* Reagill (as before), Gilshaughlin Wood 35727 52430: Brougham 35385 52915: White Ox Farm 35100 53180: Inglewood Cottage 34823 54308: High Hesket 34770 54420: Scalesceugh 34500 54939: Carleton 34260 55315: Gallows Hill 34115 55470: Carlisle cathedral 33990 55590.

Appendix 5: OS grid references of selected points on certain roads in the southern counties:
West Coggeshall to Stanway, Essex. (58400 22240) (58500 22253) (58600 22275) (58700 22295) (58800 22320) (59000 22345) (59300 22395): Marks Tey to North Witham, Essex. (59150 22365) (59000 22208) (58900 22123) (58700 21950) (58600 21860) (58500 21738) (58325 21610): Tillbridge Lane, Lincoln. (48360 38243) (48500 38170) (48700 38100) (48900 38045) (49100 37963) (49300, 37900) (49740 37750): Wragby Road, Lincoln. (49800 27190) (49900 27247) (50000 27305) (50400 27532) (50600 27623) (50700 27700) (50800 27780): Peddars' Way, Norfolk, (57100 34028) (57200 33770) (57300 33505) (57400 33237) (57700 32568) (57900 32136) (58175 31530): Woodensborough to North Dover, (63020 15670) (63100 15350) (63128 15000) (63140 14800) (63150 14700) (63160 14500) (63170 14400): Canterbury to Dover. (61500 15750) (61700 15560) (61800 15455) (61900 15330) (62000 15210) (62100 15100) (62300 14745): Honiton to Exeter. (30655 09645) (30800 09700) (31025 09810) (31245 09900) (31300 09930) (31400 09975) (31700 10105)

Appendix 6: OS grid references of points on the *limites* of the Inglewood centuriation:
Line AB, (33852 54995) (33912 54888) (33977 54788) (34110 54570) (34225 54372) (34312 54229) (34347 54180) (34449 54003) (34479 53950) (34528 53870) (34581 53772) Line EF (34055 54083) (34088 54099) (34108 54112) (34121 54117) (34148 54130) (34147 54135) (34175 54153) (34180 54145) (34265 54212) (34300 54217) (34328 54235) (34409 54279) (34457 54314) (34487 54330) (34489 54328) (34550 54361).

Appendix 7: Formulae for calculating the OS co-ordinates of an angled grid
A northing at a point *h actus* north of, and at angle Z to, a given northing N is given by N + (*h Sine* Z) having converted *h* to km. as in (2) above. Likewise, E − (*h Cosine* Z), gives an easting *h actus* west of a given co-ordinate E. An easting to the east of the given co-ordinate, is given by E + (*h Cosine* Z).

Appendix 8: Calculation for the projection of alignment 2 of the Reagill – Carlisle road
Where *h* is the length of the road line (say 30 miles), the value for *e* (difference in eastings) is given by *h*. *Sine* 26.56. The value for *n* (difference in northings) is given by *h. Cosine* 25.56. The eastings and northings for the line's end (Wall Knowe) are found by subtracting *e* from Reagill's easting by adding *n* to its northing. The lengths are converted to Roman measure as shown above.

Appendix 9: OS grid references of road alignment nodes on the Chester to York route
Chester cathedral 34065 36648: Eddisbury 35525 36920: Northwich Bridge 36565 36920: King Street (junction) 36791 37445: Holford Farm 37080 37580: Tabley House 37215 37810: Bucklow Hill Nth. 37330 38400: Crossford Bridge 37920 39310: Stretford, 38040 39575: Manchester fort 38318 39762: Castle Shaw 39985 40970: Outlane Slack 40843 41746: Holme Farm 43780 44215: Hope Hall, Bramham 44100 44280: Tadcaster Bridge 44875 44350: Hagg Wood 45475 44625: Bond Hill 45910 45850: York 46065 45220.

Appendix 10: OS eastings and northings at ten-mile intervals from OS 636.10N 143.30N, *Cantium Prom*. Figure A10 shows the lines at 20-mile intervals on the map.

miles	E	N	miles	E	N	miles	E	N
10	621.31	158.09	110	473.45	305.95	210	325.58	453.82
20	606.53	172.87	120	458.66	320.74	220	310.80	468.60
30	591.74	187.66	130	443.87	335.53	230	296.01	483.39
40	576.95	202.45	140	429.09	350.31	240	281.22	498.18
50	562.17	217.23	150	414.30	365.10	250	266.44	512.96
60	547.38	232.02	160	399.51	379.89	260	251.65	527.75
70	532.59	246.81	170	384.73	394.67	270	236.86	542.54
80	517.81	261.59	180	369.94	409.46	280	222.08	557.32
90	503.02	276.38	190	355.15	424.25	290	207.29	572.11
100	488.23	291.17	200	340.37	439.03	300	192.50	586.90

Appendix 11: Figure A11 shows how a 5 x 6 rectangle links the 3:4:5 triangle to the 3:5 triangle, providing a useful paradigm for laying out survey lines.

Appendix 12: Figure A12 shows a map with some Roman roads and towns and two planning grids; one aligned 3/5 E of N and the other 3/5 N of W(OS). The grid lines are at 60 *centuriae* intervals. Note the triangle whose apex is at Cirencester

Appendix 13: Figure A13 shows the NSEW survey grid and putative angled planning grids on the map of the province.

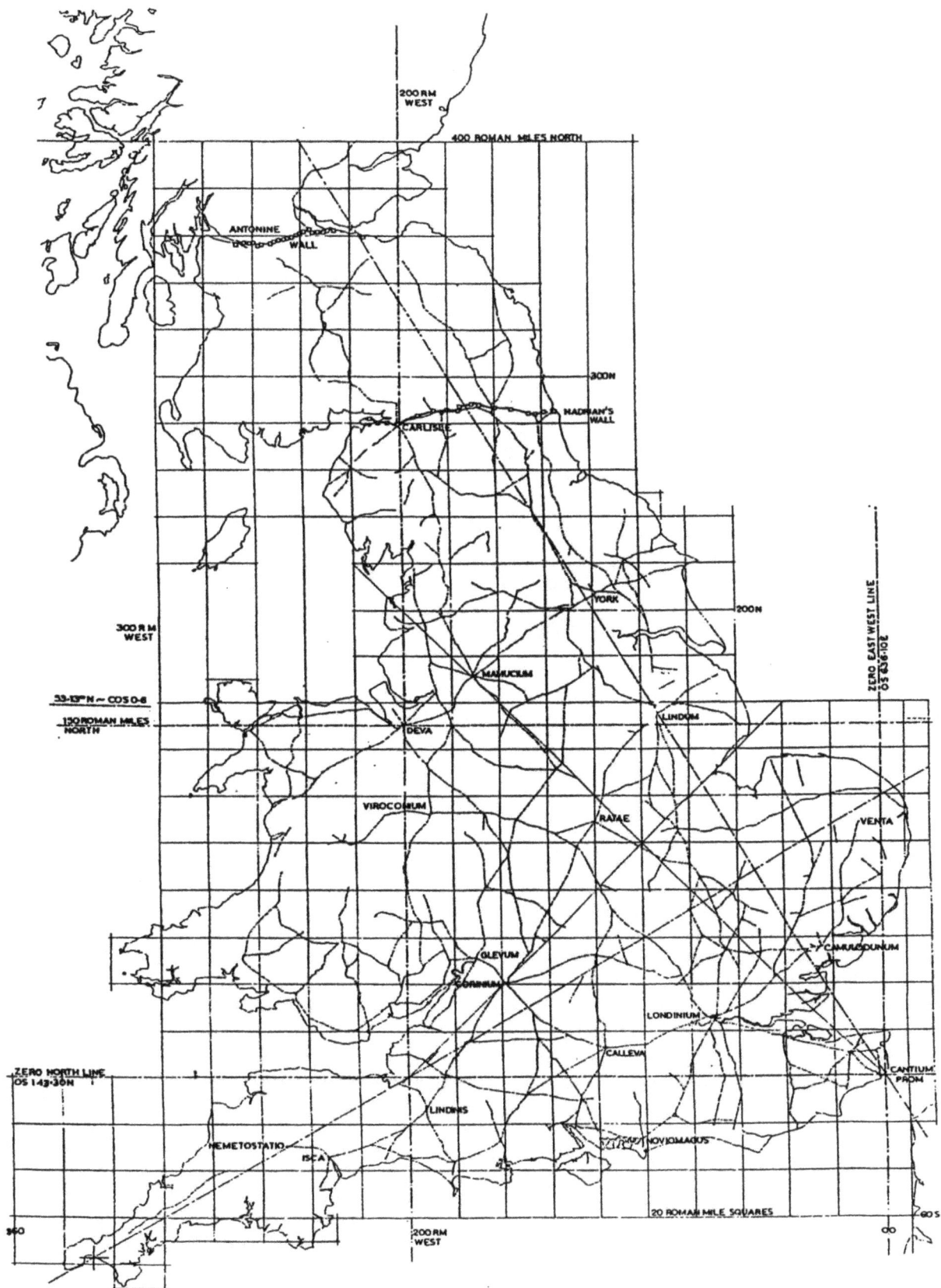

Fig A10
OS eastings and northings at 20 mile intervals from *Cantium Prom*

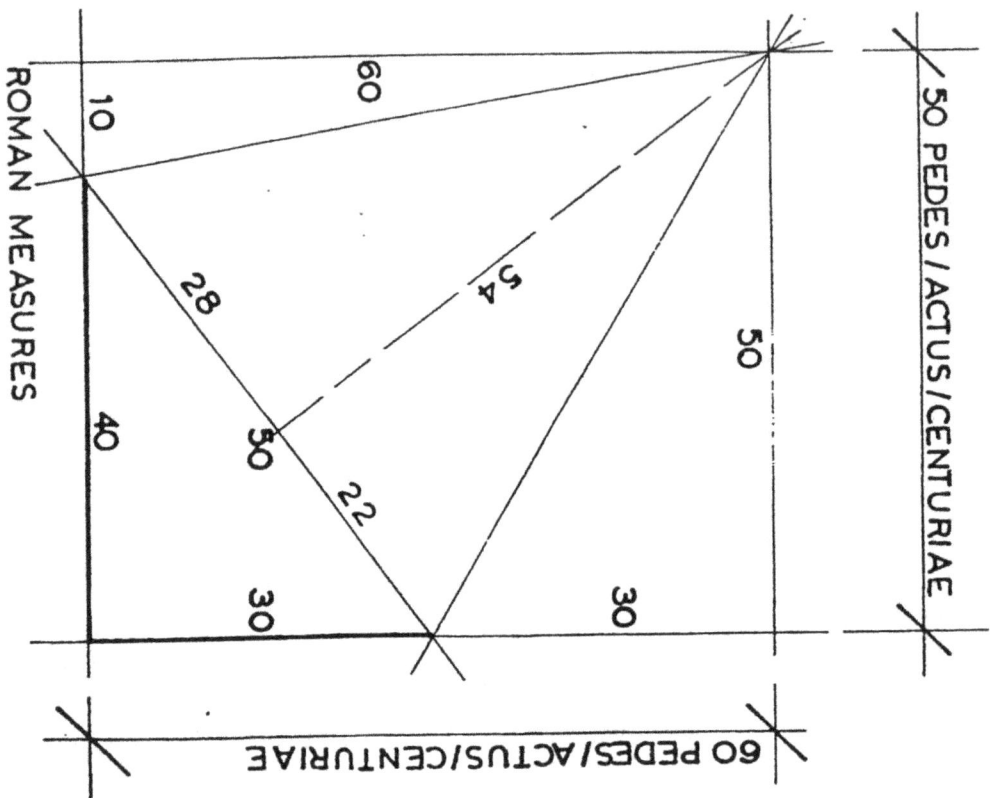

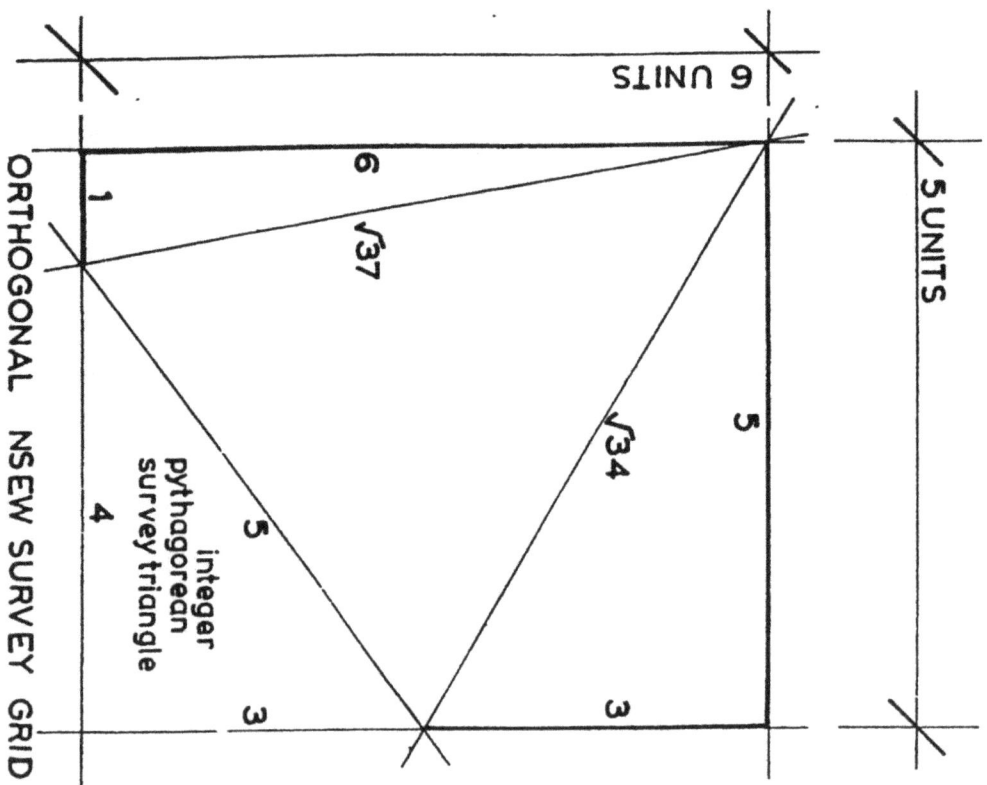

Fig A11
Geometric relationships between the 3:4:5 and 3:5 triangles
(Note how a 5 x 6 rectangle contains both triangles, providing a practical survey paradigm.)

78

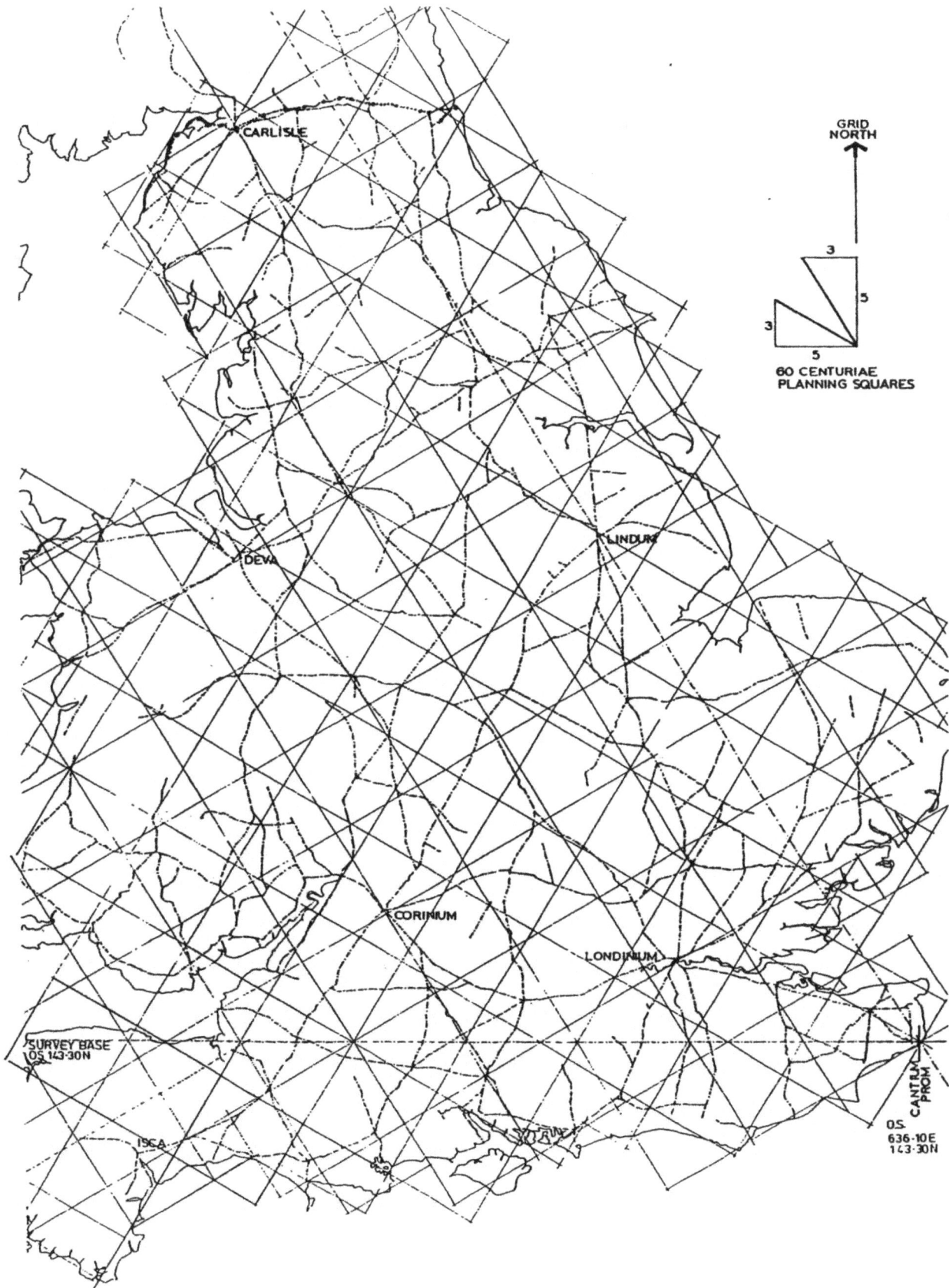

Fig A12
Map with two angled planning grids

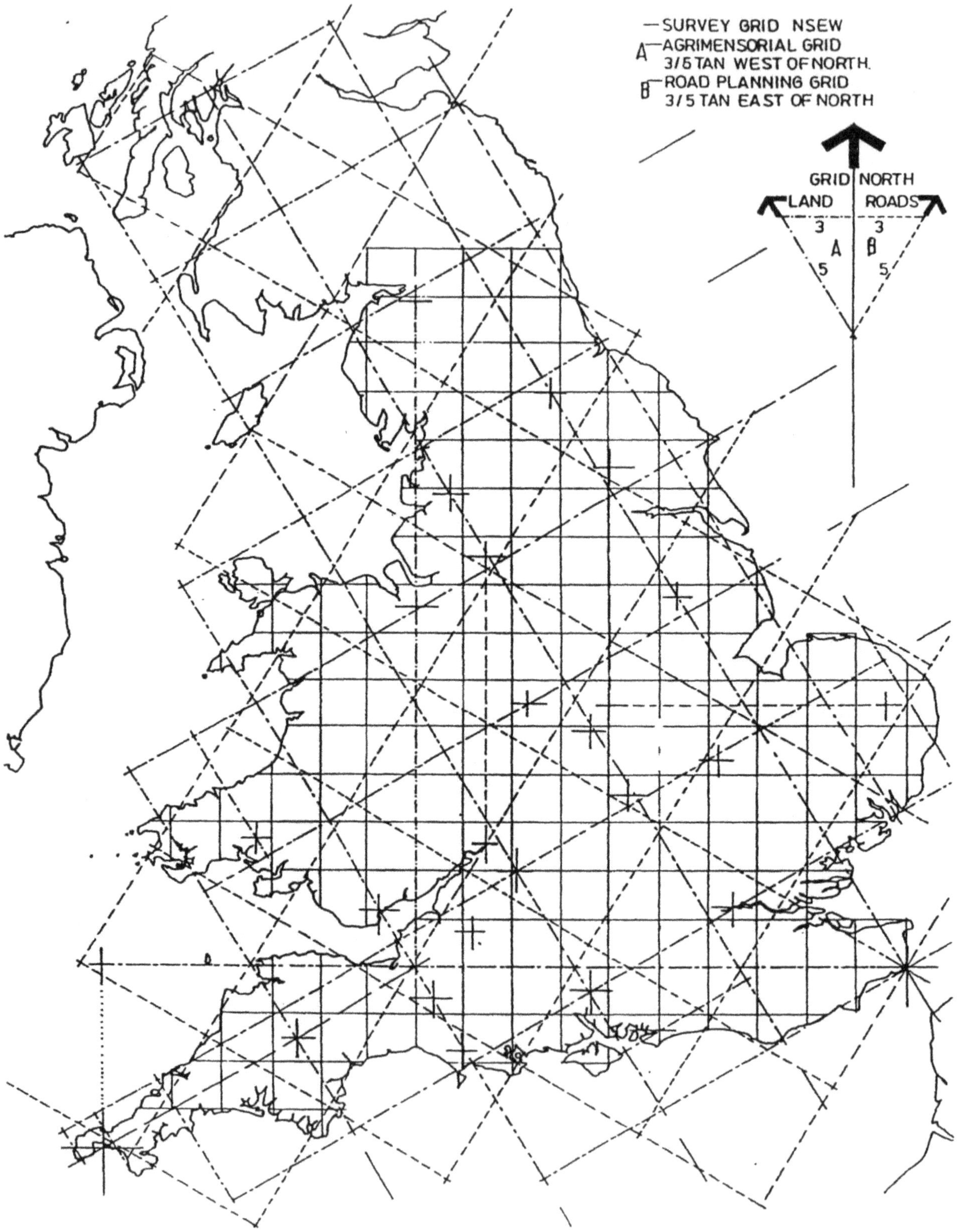
— SURVEY GRID NSEW
A — AGRIMENSORIAL GRID
3/5 TAN WEST OF NORTH.
B — ROAD PLANNING GRID
3/5 TAN EAST OF NORTH
GRID NORTH
LAND
ROADS
3
3
A
B
5
5

Fig A13
Putative angled planning grids superimposed on the NSEW grid

REFERENCES

1. Anon 1818; *Report of the Commissioners of Enclosure of the Inglewood Forest.* County Record Office, Carlisle.
2. Anon 1987: *The Encyclopaedia of Religion*, Vol. 15, McMillan, New York.
3. Anon 1995: *Roman Road, High Moor, Saddleworth*, University of Manchester Archaeological Unit, Report.
4. Anon 1996: *The Oxford Classical Dictionary*, edited by Simon Hornblower and Anthony Spawforth, 3rd Edition, Oxford.
5. Armstrong, A.M., Mawer, A., Stenton, F.M., Dickens, B., undated: *Placenames of Cumberland,* vol. xx, Cambridge.
6. Aujac. G., 1987: *The Growth of Cartography in Hellenistic Greece*, in Harley and Woodward, 1987.
7. Aujac G., 1987a: *Greek Cartography in the Early Roman World*, in Harley and Woodward, 1987.
8. Beazley, C.R., undated, *The Dawn of Modern Geography*, Vol. II, chap. 7 cited by Cary and Warmington 1963, p. 290.
9. Berryman A. E., 1953: *Historical Metrology*, J.M. Dent and Son Ltd., London.
10. Bowey, T., 1715: *Thomas Bowey's Map* DX/128/7/21, County Record Office, Carlisle.
11. Bowman, W., 1960: *England in Ashton under Lyne*, 43-46.
12. Bradford J., 1957: *Ancient Landscapes*, London, cited by Dilke (1971), 136.
13. Breeze A., 2001: Transactions of the Cumberland and Westmorland Antiquarian and Archaeological Society (Third Series), Vol. 1, 195-196.
14. Breeze D.J. and Dobson B, 1976: *Hadrian's Wall,* Allen Lane, London, 140, 155.
15. Budiansky, S., 1997: *The Nature of Horses*, Weidenfield and Nicholson, London.
16. Burdett, P.P., 1777: *A Survey of the County Palatine of Chester,* printed for the Historical Society of Lancashire and Cheshire, 1974.
17. Burn, A. R., 1965: *The Pelican History of Greece,* Penguin Books, London.
18. Campbell B., 1996: Journal of Roman Studies, LXXXVI, 74-99.
19. Caruana, I., and Coulston, J.C., 1987: *A Roman bridge stone from the River Eden, Carlisle*, Transactions of the Cumberland and Westmorland Antiquarian and Archaeological Society (Second Series), lxxxvii, 43 – 51.
20. Cary M. and Warmington E.H., 1963: *The Ancient Explorers*, Pelican Books, first published in 1929 by Methuen.
21. Chevallier R., 1976: *Roman Roads*, B.T. Batsford, London, 81.
22. Connor, R.D., 1987: *The Weights and Measures of England*, Science Museum Publications, London.
23. Crofton A., 1885: Lancashire and Cheshire Antiquarian Society, 3, 190.
24. Crofton, H.T., 1905: Lancashire and Cheshire Antiquarian Society, 23, 112-171.
25. Crump, W.B., 1939: *Saltways from the Cheshire Wiches,* Lancashire and Cheshire Antiquarian Society, Vol. LIV, 84-142.
26. Davies, H.E.H., 1998: *Designing Roman Roads*, Britannia, XXIX, 1-16.
27. Della Corte, M., 1912: III Pompeii. *Continuazione dello scavo dell'Abbondanza*, Notische degli Scavi antichita, cited by Schioler 1994.
28. De Selincourt, A., 1972: *Herodotus, The Histories*, Penguin Classics.
29. De Burgh, W.G., 1924: *The Legacy of the Ancient World*, MacDonald and Evans, London.
30. Dilke O.A.W., 1971: *The Roman Land Surveyors.* David and Charles, Newton Abbot.
31. Dilke O.A.W., 1985: *Greek and Roman Maps*, Thames and Hudson, London.
32. Diller, A., 1948: *The Ancient Measurements of the Earth*, Isis Magazine for Oxford University, Vol. XL, 6-9.
33. Dodgson J. McN., 1970: *The Place Names of Cheshire;* Part I, Cambridge, 4.
34. Dymond, D., 1985: *The Norfolk Landscape*, in *Prehistoric Landscapes*, Hodder and Stoughton, London.
35. Evans, I. H., 1990, Brewer's Dictionary of Phrase and Fable, 4th Edition, Cassel, London.
36. Esdaile, G., 1892: *Lancashire and Cheshire Antiquarian Society,* Vol. 10, 118-222.
37. Fabricius, E., 1900: *Bericht uber die Arbeiten der Reichslimeskommision in Jahre 1900,* Archaologischer Anzeiger, Berlin, cited by Schioler 1994.
38. Frere, S., 2000: *A Limitatio of Icenean Territory?* Britannia, 350-355.
39. Gossellin, P.F.J., 1883: *Systeme D' Eratosthene*, cited by Harley and Woodward (1987), 153-157.
40. Ferguson R.S., 1886: *The Beaumont Hoard,* Transactions of the Cumberland and Westmorland Antiquarian and Archaeological Society (Old Series), viii, 373 - 381.

41. Ferguson R.S., 1890: *Roman Roads,* in *History of Cumberland,* Elliot Stock, London.
42. Graham T.H.B., 1907: Transactions of the Cumberland and Westmorland Antiquarian and Archaeological Society (New Series), vii. 42-51.
43. Hall, J., 1974: *Hall's Dictionary of Subjects and Symbols in Art,* John Murray, London.
44. Handford, S.A., 1951: *Caesar: The Conquest of Gaul,* Penguin Classics, London.
45. Harley J.B. and Woodward D., 1987: *The History of Cartography, vol. 1, Cartography in Prehistoric, Ancient and Mediaeval Europe and the Mediterranean,* University of Chicago.
46. Hardie, C., 1965: *The origin and plan of Roman Florence,* Journal of Roman Studies, vol. 55, 122-140.
47. Heath, T., 1921: *A History of Greek Mathematics,* Clarendon Press, Oxford.
48. Higham N.J., 1986: Transactions of the Cumberland and Westmorland Antiquarian and Archaeological Society (New Series), lxxxvi, 85-100.
49. Higson. J., undated: *The Gorton Historical Recorder,* published by the author.
50. Hodgkinson and Donald, 1771-1774: *A Map of Cumberland,* County Record Office Carlisle.
51. Hogg, R., 1952: *The historic crossings of the River Eden at Stanwix and their associated road system,* Transactions of the Cumberland and Westmorland Antiquarian and Archaeological Society (New Series), lii, 1131 – 159.
52. Humphries A.B., 1993: *Agrarian Change in East Cumberland 1750-1900,* M. Phil. Thesis, University of Lancaster, 15.
53. Hutchinson, W., 1794-97: *A History of the County of Cumberland,* Vol. 1, Carlisle.
54. MacDonald, G., 1934: *The Roman Wall in Scotland,* Oxford.
55. McGillivray H., (undated), *A History of the Parish of Hesket in the Forest,* an unpublished MS, County Record Office, Carlisle.
56. Manning W.H., 1975: *Economic influences on land use in the military areas of the Highland Zone during the Roman period,* in *The Effect of Man on the Landscape: Highland Zone,* The Council for British Archaeology, Research Rep. No. 11, 112-116.
57. Margary I.D., 1954 -57: *Roman Roads in Britain,* Phoenix House Ltd., London.
58. Mayr-Harting, H., 1977: *The Coming of Christianity to Anglo-Saxon England,* Book Club Associates, London.
59. Melland, C.H., 1936: Journal of the Manchester Geographical Society, lxvi, 59-62.
60. Middleton, T., 1936: *The History of Denton and Haughton,* cited by Nevell M., 1992, 96.
61. Middleton, T., 1906: *The Annals of Hyde and District,* reprinted by Longden Publications, 1973.
62. Nevell, M., 1992: *Tameside before 1066,* Tameside Metropolitan Borough Council, 80.
63. Peterson, J.M.W., 1988: *Roman cadastres in Britain: 1- South Norfolk A.,* Dialogues d'histoire ancienne, 14, 167-199.
64. Peterson, J.M.W., 1998: *South Norfolk "A".* In *Atlas Historique des cadastres d'Europe. Royaume Uni,* Dossier 1 edited by Clavel-Leveque, M. and Vignot, A., 1-10. Office for Official Publications of the European Community, Luxembourg.
65. Peterson, J.M.W., in press: *Kent "A".* In *Atlas Historique des cadastres d'Europe. Royaume Uni,* Dossier 2., edited by Clavel-Leveque, M. and Orejas, A., Office for Official Publications of the European Community, Luxembourg.
66. Petrikovits H. von, 1960: *Das romische Rheinland Archaologische Forschungen seit 1945,* Koln und Opladen: Westdeutscher Verlag, cited by Manning (1975).
67. Piggott, S., 1992: *Wagon, Chariot and Carriage: Symbol and Status,* in *The History of Transport,* Thames and Hudson, New York, cited by Budiansky S., (1997).
68. Radice, B., 1978: *The Personal Letters,* Book 10, 17b, in *Pliny, A Self Portrait in Letters,* The Folio Society, London, 1978, 213.
69. Richardson, A., 1982: *Evidence of centuriation in the Inglewood Forest,* Transactions of the Cumberland and Westmorland Antiquarian and Archaeological Society (New Series), lxxxii, 67-71.
70. Richardson, A., 1983: *Evidence of Roman Centuriation at Manchester,* Cheshire Archaeological Bulletin, 9, 9-17.
71. Richardson, A., 1984: *An old road in the Eden valley,* Transactions of the Cumberland and Westmorland Antiquarian and Archaeological Society (New Series), lxxxiv, 79 – 83.
72. Richardson, A., 1986: *Further evidence of centuriation in Cumbria,* Transactions of the Cumberland and Westmorland Antiquarian and Archaeological Society (New Series), lxxxvi, 71-78.
73. Richardson, A., 1986: *Further Evidence of Centuriation at Manchester,* The Manchester Geographer, Vol. 7, 44-50.
74. Richardson, A., 1996: *Centuriation south of Hadrian's Wall in Cumberland,* Yearbook and Transactions of the Matterdale Historical and Archaeological Society, (ISSN 1367 6857), 5, 7-14.

75. Richardson, A., 2000: *The numerical basis of Roman camps*, Oxford Journal of Archaeology, 19, No 4, 425-437.
76. Richardson, A., 2001: *The order of battle in the Roman army: Evidence from marching camps,* Oxford Journal of Archaeology, 20, No2, 171-185.
77. Ross P., 1918: *The Roman Road from Ilkley to Aldborough,* Bradford Antiquary, VI, part 20, 279-302.
78. Ross P., 1920: *The Roman Road north of Low Borrow Bridge, to Brougham Castle, Westmoreland,* Transactions of the Cumberland and Westmorland Antiquarian and Archaeological Society (New Series), xx, 1 –15.
79. Sauer, E., 2001: *Roman Alchester,* Current Archaeology, No 173, 189 -191.
80. Schioler, T., 1994: *The Pompeii groma in New Light,* Analecta Romana, Instituti Danici, XXII. Rome.
81. Selkirk, R., 1983: *The Piercebridge Formula,* Patrick Stephen, and Cambridge.
82. Speake R. and Witty F.R., 1953: *A History of Droylsden,* Cloister Press, Stockport.
83. Stevenson, L., 1932: *Ptolemy Claudius, the Geography,* New York.
84. Summerson, H., 1991: *Murder at Hutton in the Forest: A study in the government of thirteenth century Cumberland,* Transactions of the Cumberland and Westmorland Antiquarian and Archaeological Society (New Series), xci, 59-68.
85. Williamson, T., 1987: *Early Co-axial Field Systems on the East Anglian Boulder Clays,* Proceedings of the Prehistoric Society, 53, 419 – 431.
86. Wilson P.A., 1976: *Brougham Castle and early communications in the Eden valley,* Transactions of the Cumberland and Westmorland Antiquarian and Archaeological Society (New Series), lxxvii, 67-76.

www.ingramcontent.com/pod-product-compliance
Lightning Source LLC
Chambersburg PA
CBHW061303270326
41932CB00029B/3448